# TIME
# AND
# FESTIVITY

# TIME
# AND
# FESTIVITY

## ESSAYS ON MYTH AND LITERATURE

## FURIO JESI

EDITED BY ANDREA CAVALLETTI
TRANSLATED BY CRISTINA VITI

LONDON NEW YORK CALCUTTA

*The Italian List*
SERIES EDITOR: ALBERTO TOSCANO

Seagull Books, 2021

Originally published as Furio Jesi, *Il tempo della festa* in 2011 by
Nottetempo srl, Italy. © Nottetempo srl, 2011

English translation © Cristina Viti, 2021

First published in English by Seagull Books, 2021

The translator would like to thank Kieran Aarons for publishing
'A Reading of Rimbaud's "Bateau ivre"' in *Theory & Event* 22(4)
(October 2019).

ISBN   978 0 8574 2 630 7

**British Library Cataloguing-in-Publication Data**
A catalogue record for this book is available
from the British Library

Typeset by Seagull Books, Calcutta, India
Printed and bound by Hyam Enterprises, Calcutta, India

# CONTENTS

# Festivity, Writing and Destruction

ANDREA CAVALLETTI

The essays presented in this book are among Furio Jesi's least known, or among the few that have so far remained unpublished; but they are also some of the best and most substantial he ever wrote. We have chosen to collect them here in an attempt to offer the reader a faithful image of the great scholar, and especially of what was perhaps the most fruitful period of his production, following the break with his teacher Károly Kerényi and the writing of *Spartakus: The Symbology of Revolt*,[1] which he completed in December 1969. This period was crucially marked by the introduction of the 'mythological machine model' (1972), the theoretical device that makes Jesi's thought so urgently relevant to our times, showing equal effectiveness whether it is applied to the science of myth and anthropology or to philosophy and political praxis. In addition to 'A Reading of Rimbaud's "Bateau ivre"' and 'Knowability of the Festival' (the texts more strictly connected to the 'machine' and its articulations), we have included three essays by which he paid homage to some of the most influential figures in his constellation: Rilke, the poet he studied and translated throughout his life

---

1 Furio Jesi, *Spartakus. Simbologia della rivolta* (Turin: Bollati Boringhieri, 2000) / *Spartakus: The Symbology of Revolt* (Andrea Cavalletti ed., Alberto Toscano trans.) (London: Seagull Books, 2014). [Trans.]

(we are presenting an introduction to the *Duino Elegies* written around 1977); young Lukács (along with Kierkegaard), the subject of the 'descant' to the text of *Spartakus*; and Cesare Pavese, revisited by Jesi a decade after his first essay (published in 1964) in pages leavened by a strong autobiographical tone and a touch of subtle humour. These names are also joined by those of Kerényi—resonating, whether openly or implicitly, on almost every page—and Benjamin, on whom Jesi had intended to write a monograph in the early 1970s: in 'Knowability of the Festival', Benjamin's *Theses on the Philosophy of History* are not only quoted and discussed, but also, beginning with the title, evoked in their best-known form (*das Jetzt der Erkennbarkeit*, 'the now of knowability').

Alongside these great early texts, we have included a self-portrait in the form of an interview, in which Jesi retraces the stepping stones of his life as a scholar— from his beginnings as an Egyptologist when he was just fifteen to the writing of *Materiali mitologici*[2] and his long-standing work on Bachofen—and recalls among other things his first Jungian readings, his early distancing from Jung and closer connection with Kerényi.

An important, hitherto unpublished essay on the Book of Daniel will reveal to the reader an unknown aspect of Jesi's work. Probably written before the elaboration of the 'mythological machine', it marks one of the late developments of the model based on 'archetypal connections' (the elements structuring mythological language as an 'autonomous internal circulation peculiar

---

2 Furio Jesi, *Materiali mitologici* (Turin: Einaudi, 2001[1979]). [Trans.]

to certain materials'). It is also, and above all, an essay in which Jesi, for once directly, investigates down to the subtlest details and deepest connections a document belonging to the Jewish tradition, taking the Talmudic commentaries as a starting point for long explorations into extra-Jewish literatures and into the distant (and, to him, well known) lands of Greece and Egypt. It is a reading of the Story of Susanna: a text connected with the condition of exile and bilingualism of the Hellenistic Jews, and positioned by Jesi in a 'space of indeterminacy as to familiarity vs foreignness'; form vs formlessness; licit vs illicit.

In this respect we should do well to remember that in 1970 Jesi had published a collection of poems, *L'esilio*,[3] connecting its title to 'the distinct developments of the concept of "exile" in the Jewish cultural and religious tradition': clearly significant words, which we might want to read together with those found in a manuscript dated 10 February 1961 and held by Marta Rossi Jesi: 'All I have written is *poetry*.'

The statute of writing and its connection with the dimension of exile can however be investigated on the basis of a passage in a letter Jesi wrote to Gershom Scholem at the end of 1966: 'I have found that my atheism increasingly turns into a hesitation to name the darkness I perceive in the depths of being—into the refusal of a naming that appears blasphemous to me.'[4] This hesitation,

---

3 Furio Jesi, *L'esilio* (Rome: Silva, 1970). [Trans.]
4 I am able to quote this passage thanks to the courtesy of Enrico Lucca, who found this letter in the Scholem Archive in Jerusalem. An Italian translation of the letter, originally written in French, was published in

which is the stance taken when facing the exile of the deity ('God is darkness, and I want to be silent'), and which by turning into a refusal perfectly matches the unutterability of the Name, thus seems to be for Jesi, 'the son of a Jewish man and a Christian woman, raised in a Christian cultural environment', the connection between Jewish orthodoxy and atheism, the latter seen as a form of recusance of any possible hypostasis (Jesi once wrote, advisedly quoting a well-known Kabbalistic formula transmitted by Scholem: 'I am not a Christian precisely because I refuse with sincere repugnance a God that is not *Gott als ganz Anderes* to the point of exiling himself "in the depths of his own nothingness"').

Clearly this is not the place to tackle the complex question of Jesi's relationship with his Jewish heritage. It is however appropriate to note that everything Jesi wrote, whether as a mythologist or as a historian of religions, is poetry—in that it is a relationship with a myth or a deity such as can only arise in a situation of exile; and as Jesi explains in the interview that closes this volume, 'to know', in exile, means to abide by the terms of a constant and paradoxical apprenticeship: it means 'learn[ing] [ . . . ] to *not* know' myth—and not name it.

Kerényi had always 'sought, as a so-called mythologist, to completely avoid uttering the word "myth"', by then already synonymous with falsehood, while nonetheless working on myth narratives and mythologies; and finally, during a famous conference held in Rome in

---

'Dossier Jesi. Lettere e materiali (Furio Jesi, Gershom Scholem)', *Scienza & Politica* 25(48) (2013): 103–109. [Available online at: bityl.co/3lmy (last accessed 1 July 2020).]

1964, he made 'an attempt to find a way out of this ambiguity and confusion' by distinguishing inauthentic myth, which is dangerously 'technicized' (reduced that is to an instrument of political power), from 'genuine myth' as the 'original phenomenon' (*Urphä-nomen*) spontaneously arising in man and forming the basis of all mythologies.[5] Jesi radicalizes this position: mythologies are not in his view derived from myth but, rather, produced by a machine that only alludes to the existence of myth as origin, as the core that remains hidden behind the walls of the machine itself. If a mythologist today can study and analyse mythologies as historically appreciable products, when faced with the problem of the existence of myth she can only hesitate: any attempt to name that origin, any word marked with *Ur-* and *Arche-*, can only cause her to feel a sincere repugnance.

There is a clear connection between Jesi's 'Reading of the "Bateau ivre"' and his 'Knowability of the Festival': they are in fact respectively the first and last of the theoretical texts written over a four-year span on the 'mythological machine'. The elaboration of this model cannot however be separated from the special composition technique that Jesi had been refining over the years. True, his essays had been conceived as single pieces, and were sometimes written on an occasional basis: but that is precisely the reason why they had, right from the outset, the character of fragments endowed with a potential affinity, and

---

5 See the 'Discussion' following Kerényi's conference 'Dal mito genuino al mito tecnicizzato' in *Archivio di Filosofia* (1964): 163–4. The expression *echter Mythos* ('genuine myth'), used by Kerényi in a particular acceptation connected to Goethe's *Urphänomen*, is actually due to Walter F. Otto.

therefore with a yet-latent legibility, that would only be revealed at the moment of their being collected and composed into a volume. If Jesi really was one of the great essayists of the twentieth century, if we can say that the essay form shone through him as it did through Lukács, through Adorno, through Benjamin, it is because, like the first two, he succeeded in practising it while also making it a privileged subject of reflection, and like the latter—the one he was closest to—he also saw it as a modality of 'knowledge by composition'. Jesi would write even the most arduous texts straight out, typing them directly in their final version; but he would give much thought to the table of contents of each collection—just like Benjamin, in his final years, would organize his work through the long and troubled phase of his 'director's notes', the preliminary framework of guidelines for the montage of his materials. And if Jesi's essays are compositions of quotations, then his books are compositions of essays which have been given the role previously played by quotations. Entirely made of fragments, his books are therefore totally quotable essays.

Thus some of the salient findings in *Spartakus* appear in the 'Reading of the "Bateau ivre"' which opens our selection. If the book was not a history of the Spartacist movement but rather a 'phenomenology of revolt'—if 1968 Paris as Jesi knew it was transfigured in those pages to become 1919 Berlin, here it is Berlin that reverts to being Paris as the barricades of May 1968 are superimposed onto those of the Commune. And the themes central to *Spartakus* unfold according to a pattern consistent with Rimbaud's poem. It would thus be appropriate to reread *Spartakus* on the basis of its later offshoots: the 'Reading of the "Bateau ivre"', 'Know-ability of the Festival' and equally the pages Jesi wrote with great clarity on the theme of sacrifice in 'Cesare Pavese and Myth. *Dix ans plus tard*', or his text on young Lukács. Likewise it is appropriate to return to *Spartakus*, Jesi's first, powerful reflection on the problem of myth as a problem of time.

In those pages, written in 1969, the only possible apparition of genuine myth as a truly shared experience coincided with the 'suspension' of historical time in the moment of revolt. Revolt—which Jesi (in a passage he later reprised in the essay on Rimbaud) distinguished from 'revolution', a process deep *within* the flow of history—was the destruction of the symbols of domination, an instant of truth and knowledge, the collective sharing into the epiphany of the idea. But it was also an unconscious yielding to some of the mythologies orchestrated by power: to see the enemy as an 'inhuman monster' meant being subjugated by the fascination of a figure deployed by the Great War, it meant being made to oppose the enemy by a behaviour that was 'human' to the point of self-sacrifice, thus endowing that monster with actual power. Revolt was thus only an interlude, at the end of which the 'bourgeois manipulation of time' (Jesi's translation of the Kerényian concept of 'techni-cization') could reinstate its typical product, so-called normal time, parcelled out in work timetables and enforced pauses. 'When everything was over, some of the protagonists had left the scene for ever', and with their sacrifice 'memory and continuity' took over from 'epiphany and subversion'. The apparition of myth, the novelty of the idea, the suspension of historical time even, thus remained circumscribed 'by precise borders traced in historical time and historical space', and it was in fact a death rite that locked the circle shut.

The crucial experiment in *Spartakus* consisted of the attempt to escape the mythologies that work their spell on insurgents past and present, to think oneself out of the vicious circle of 'great sacrificers' and 'great victims', the functional opposition separating the stilled time or eternal present of myth from the flow of history. Accordingly, Jesi proposed an astonishing philosophy of subjectivity, a theory of the 'double Sophia', or of consciousness as the common denominator between the worlds of history and myth. The 'I' saved from sacrifice is neither the one glorified in the images of the hero (as in Rosa Luxemburg and Karl Liebknecht within certain Expressionist stage settings)—nor, clearly, the one who survives by chance or escapes the battle to rejoin the ranks of bourgeois society. For Jesi, the saved 'I' is the one who can escape the conniving game of myth vs history, positioning itself exactly at their intersection and 'knowing at one and the same time [ . . . ] permanence and self-destruction, historical time and myth time'. It is 'the common element, the point of intersection between two universes [ . . . ], that is subject to historical time while being part of mythical time'; or again, with the Rilkean formula much loved by Kerényi, it is the 'I' who 'in the instant of its access to myth "pours forth like a spring", destroys itself in a dynamic process that involves its own historical duration. In short, the I is truly part of the flow of history when it succeeds in identifying with that flow the course of its own destruction, and hence its own access to myth.'

Just as myth does not remain outside history, so too the real unfolding of history cannot in this perspective be isolated from myth: rather, it is the process through which the 'I' is destroyed by coming into contact with myth.

The category of *destruction*, that since Bakunin at least has defined the essence of the insurrectional phenomenon, and that was connected to the category of justice in Benjamin's 'messianic anarchism', is thus the subject of an entirely original rethinking in the 'phenomenology of revolt'. If, in the language of Jesi the mythologist (and since such early essays as the one on Rilke and Egypt he wrote in 1964)[6], destruction of the self does not in fact stand for death as the end of life but, rather, loss of the limits of the individual 'I' in the encounter with myth as 'eternity present in man's life', in *Spartakus* this encounter is invested with a political significance: it corresponds to an act of insurrection that can be understood not as sacrifice of one's life but as sacrifice and the self-destruction of the subject's bourgeois components, into access to the newness and otherness of myth time. This is the decisive step of the demythologizing challenge that Jesi drives against the lure of technicized images. Set free from the mythologies of heroic death and from the victim/sacrificer bind, revolt is urgent, here and now, beyond the time and space boundaries locked shut by that bind and by those mythologies: the actual writing of *Spartakus* becomes in itself the instant of 'ceaseless battle'.

---

6 Furio Jesi, 'Rilke e l'Egitto. Considerazioni sulla X Elegia di Duino', *Aegyptus* 4(1964): 58–65; subsequently in *Letteratura e mito* (Turin: Einaudi, 2002[1968]). [Trans.]

From the destruction of those boundaries, *Spartakus* continues and echoes through many of these essays: materially extending and conceptually developing primarily into the 'Reading of the "Bateau ivre"'. The dialectic between absolute novelty and crystallization of the idea, that had opened the 1969 book, returns in the first paragraph of the essay, and is set out in terms of the novelty par excellence of the poetic operation vs the non-novelty of the commonplace; the concept of the mythical epiphany as a time that is 'other' and a 'suspension of historical time' returns in the central paragraphs (p. 35 in this volume), that are in a very real sense grafted onto some pages from *Spartakus*. And as in a variation on the same musical theme, the 'mythological machine model' now takes over from the concept of 'bourgeois manipulation of time'. The machine keeps myth constantly separate from history, and in doing so gives us to understand that poetry's linguistic formulations *come* to us from an 'other' world. Like myths, the 'commonplaces' to which young Rimbaud has recourse—so as to make poetry into a merchandise that can be appreciated by adults while at the same time preparing his revolt against them—'are first and foremost what a creative experience presses us to believe exists while also keeping its essence well concealed [ . . . ]. To believe this is tantamount to believing that myth exists autonomously inside the mythological machine, which is situated—as the machine itself would have us believe—at the boundary between the two worlds'.

To believe in these myths or commonplaces, to believe that non-novelty was originally novelty, to believe what '*not-is there*', to become engaged in a revolt (albeit a personal one, like Rimbaud's), means giving in to the machine's deception. Yet neither is the functioning of the mechanism contradicted by the attitude of 'non-faith' taken by those who, like the revolutionary, do not believe in the existence of myth and stick close to so-called history: 'There is no more exact faith in an "other world" that *not-is there* than the declaration that such "other world" is *not*'. Revolt and revolution are but 'different articulations [ . . . ] of the time obtaining inside that box'.

So is there no chance of a way out? In the 'Bateau ivre' essay, a solution is outlined: to stop the machine, 'to sever the root of time', as Jesi puts it, 'would mean to have available a language or a set of gestures such as to face the mythological machine on a plane that would enable one to declare at the same time the existence and non-existence of what the machine purports to be containing'.

We can clearly recognize here the logic of the 'double Sophia'; and it is equally clear, on the other hand, that by producing 'commonplaces', inducing us to believe that it has installed itself 'at the boundary between the two worlds', the machine tends to usurp the place reserved for the 'I' in *Spartakus* ('the common element, the point of intersection, between two universes'). In 'Knowability of the Festival', the splendid essay that tests the model in the field of anthropology and the time of revolt in the experience of festive time, the problem is set out in the following terms:

> Machines seem to purport to contain inaccessible realities; but we cannot exclude that precisely

that might be their cunning [ . . . ]: alluding to an immoveable prime mover, in order to be disbelieved, thus inducing belief solely in them, in machines, voids, barriers built from productive mechanisms isolating one from what does not produce, until the latter is rendered apparently non-existent.

It is through this 'cunning' that machines definitively install themselves at the 'point of intersection' between history and myth, disempowering the conscious subject and reducing him to the position of a (useful and productive) subject of normalization.

But in order to discover whether this cunning of machines is truly such, and whether, beyond them, what does not produce actually *is*, it is necessary to destroy not machines themselves, which would reform like the heads of the Hydra, but rather the situation that makes machines real and productive.

In that sense, 'the gnoseological problem cannot be isolated, made autonomous, separated from the political and social problem'. For this destruction—this festival, this revolt—to endure, mythology must become concrete political experimentation, while political action must become ceaseless mythological critique: 'Destroying the situation that makes machines [ . . . ] real and productive means [ . . . ] pushing beyond the boundaries of bourgeois culture, not just trying to slightly deform its border barriers.'

These boundaries, the walls of the box, correspond to the social dominants of historical time. Pushing beyond them means, as in *Spartakus*, engaging in a ceaseless battle: here too, Jesi remains faithful to the principle he had once set out in respect to his *L'esilio*, according to which 'the battle, as long as it endures, for the very fact that it endures, is itself a sort of victory' and 'the darkest moment would be the one in which, the battle having ended, we should be forced to say "An hour has passed."'[7] Battle, festival, revolt are synonymous with one another, whereas 'duration' is synonymous with 'destruction': 'enduring', 'pushing beyond the boundaries', means identifying historical time with the 'course of destruction'.

Moments of one seamless act of writing that proceeds at the same time by soundings and by increasingly close investigations, the essays in this volume are thorough inspections of the barriers erected by the machine, or of the 'modalities of non-knowledge' of myth, and at the same time analyses of the workings of the machine: they investigate the segregations instated and maintained by the machine between 'the civilized' and 'the *others*', between adults and children or 'savages', between the conditions of vision and non-vision (including even their coexistence in the same observing subject); thus they look at the divisions governing the relationship between those who have power, and corresponding ethics, and those who don't—hence between those who have only

---

7 See Furio Jesi's letter to Giulio Schiavoni, dated 4 May 1970, in Giorgio Agamben and Andrea Cavalletti (eds), *Cultura tedesca* 12 (December 1999): 175. 'This is it, one hour has passed' are the final words in Jesi's novel *L'ultima notte*, written at the same time as *Spartakus* and published posthumously by Marietti in 1987.

years ('for those who have power, years are counted, just as they are counted—in reverse—when in prison') and those like the old or the adolescent, who on the other hand, being devoid of power, have only an age ('Adolescence and old age are conquests over time [ . . . ] that find within themselves their own atemporal norm'). They are also studies of lives and works made exemplary by the contact with the sphere of insurrection or adolescence and at the same time by exit from that sphere, whether towards a solitary revolution (Rimbaud) or towards the years of maturity and power (Lukács); studies that, again on the trail opened by *Spartakus* (an analysis of the heredities of bourgeois morals in the behaviour of insurgents), reveal and expose (in the case of young Lukács) 'the fracture through which ethics breaks into the age of adolescence'. And they are investigations into the modalities by which bourgeois culture and society prevent the identification between destruction and the flow of history: by precluding the 'dying in someone' as a vital self-destruction in the other—'*in* the loved one (not *in front of* the loved one)', as Jesi writes in *Kierkegaard*;[8] by conversely allowing *death*, which each must face alone, and again by isolating the subject as such under the sign of this death that is solitary by definition. They are also clear elucidations of the aporia faced by those who, like Pavese, come into contact with the language of myth and nature and suffer the solitude of that contact, which is singly possible but at the same time impossible for the collective: the poet, as Jesi explains, has no way left but that of sacrifice, the *religio mortis* as

---

8 Furio Jesi, *Kierkegaard* (Turin: Bollati Boringhieri, 2001[1972]). [Trans.]

an acceptance of the 'only myth in which the individual can be alone in his relationship with the language of myths, and nonetheless connected to his community'. They are, finally, explorations that push as far as shedding light on a different response to the same aporia, as in the case of the *Duino Elegies*. Faced with the impossibility of the perfect destruction of the self into myth (a destruction that would be perfect were it not solitary) and of the silence that would ensue; faced with the impossibility of making oneself into a 'blind and pure instrument of the unknowable', with the residue of individual volition opposing that transformation, Rilke would operate a systematic emptying out of all linguistic formulae (a process in some ways similar to the use of commonplaces in Rimbaud), bringing them to coincide with the pure and simple will to speak. The remnant of volition, a residue of the poet's individuality, is thus transformed from an obstacle to silence into a naked, nameless will that can coincide with the will of the unknowable.

We have recalled here a sentence from one of Jesi's early manuscripts: 'All I have written is *poetry*.' One might want to ask whether the figures of Pavese, Rilke or Rimbaud may thus not be ephemeral masks for the mythologist's face to shine through. But we have until now omitted to quote some other, conclusive words also found in those sheets dated 10 February 1961:

> [...] the poet is endowed from birth with a distortion of insight such as has him believe that without the magic words he will never attain knowledge of the secrets of the world, perhaps

never even attain self-destruction. It is indeed a distortion, for that is not the truth: in order to arrive at the desired point, simple love is enough [ . . . ]. The strange images, the mysterious stories contained in my poems are those of the secret forces that move the matter of life, constitute that matter itself.

Only these can find their way into a poem, for they are the living matter of *self-destruction*, and are in fact entirely invested by its allure.

Now that I have stopped writing and have therefore nothing more to do with magic words, my works can become positive and useful in the great final battle, as weapons and steadfast presences [ . . . ]. And besides, they no longer pose any danger, since I have stopped writing.

They should however be seen as weapons, and as such must not be published.

Since that 10 February, the names of the poets Pavese, Rilke, Rimbaud could no longer coincide with that of Jesi. Since then, the writing of one who has ceased to write, the writing from a condition of exile—the writing of *L'esilio* itself—is *poetry* and at once (if only because of being destined for publication) non-writing or *no longer pure poetry*. In this condition, stripped bare of magic, in which mythological machines have replaced myths, those poets offer weapons through which the battle can endure-win, for they 'allow an exceptional rising of consciousness'. In Jesi's essays those poets *exhibit* their weapons as steadfast presences: Pavese, perhaps the closest to him as well as the most distant, sheds a dazzling (albeit, for one who has stopped writing, harmless) light on that distortion both of the poetic insight and of the solitary commerce with magic words that is the *religio mortis*; Rilke offers the model of a writing arrayed at the intersection between history and the unknowable; and Rimbaud illustrates the trajectory from novelty to non-novelty, or the actualizing of the commonplaces, of the merchandise-poetry written 'to show people in Paris'. The poets offer their weapons, and in this display Jesi's exiled poetry is made knowable by non-coincidence: if the emerging traits of those writings do show the paradigm of the critical operation, precisely the latter remains, as 'the thinnest film', a piece of evidence that cannot be discarded, an impurity by now anonymous and still open to examination.

Mythology must become concrete political experimentation while political action must become ceaseless mythological critique. So that the battle can *endure*, the critique must however be truly ceaseless: that is, it must be 'first and foremost a critique of oneself'. So as to stop machines reconstituting themselves 'like the heads of the Hydra', to stop the machine the scholar has investigated, dissected and apparently decommissioned being reabsorbed into the mythological materials of a more powerful, as-yet-unknown device, that model must be 'simultaneously an object of knowledge and a mode of knowing'. Attaining this simultaneity means exposing, within the object, the overlaying film of the cognitive model. It means, in fact, 'declaring at the same time the existence and non-existence of what the machine purports to be containing'. *At the same time*: one time, a time of exile, of festivity and of destruction.

*

I am grateful to Marta Rossi Jesi who for fifteen years now has patiently followed my work on the writings left by Furio Jesi.

I also wish to thank Enrico Lucca and Giulio Schiavoni for their precious collaboration, as well as friends Roberto Andreotti and Federico De Melis for giving space in the pages of *Alias* magazine to the interview that closes this volume prior to its publication, and for inventing its title, 'When Kerényi Diverted Me from Jung'.

# A Reading of Rimbaud's 'Bateau ivre'

EDITOR'S NOTE

Jesi opens his important early essay *Le connessioni archetipiche*[1] with these words: 'In examining folkloristic materials from various sources, and especially compositions in popular literature, one perceives the constant presence of "commonplaces": motifs that are repeated in the different forms through which we apprehend each story, at times remaining formally unaltered, at times being modified'. In his note to *L'esilio*, he claims 'the usability of each poetic "precedent" as a repertoire of anonymous commonplaces'. And finally, in a letter to Giulio Schiavoni dated 31 October 1972, he writes: 'I'm in the middle of an essay on Rimbaud, on the "Bateau ivre" to be precise [ . . . ]. I've long had outstanding business with the "commonplace", and this might be the time for a reckoning.'

Such 'reckoning' was made possible by the elaboration of the 'mythological machine model' appearing for the first time in the following essay; but this was also the time for Jesi's reckoning with his own book *Spartakus*, written in 1969 and long left unpublished owing to unfortunate circumstances (it would be printed posthumously by Bollati Boringhieri, as late as 2000). Jesi includes in this essay some pages taken *verbatim* from the book, and develops its central themes starting from the new orientation given by the mythological machine. 'A Reading of Rimbaud's "Bateau ivre"' was first published in the magazine *Comunità* (168, 1972).

---

1 Furio Jesi, 'Le connessioni archetipiche', *Archivio internazionale di etnografia e preistoria* 1 (1958): 35–44. [Trans.]

# A Reading of Rimbaud's 'Bateau ivre'

1. Some works of art have the privilege of being made out of the matter of commonplaces and of themselves becoming a commonplace on the surface of an artist's creation. In these works, the apparent progress from the novelty par excellence of the *in flagranti* creative operation to the non-novelty par excellence of the statue erected by posterity to the creator is in fact enclosed in a single point: a sort of dark pustule on the marble surface, in which all the impurities of the stone are gathered—a salient blemish, a reference point. It is not true that the artist has taken possession of the commonplaces and made use of them. Rather, he has opened himself to them, put herself at their disposal: they have come, they have taken possession of the creative experience and made use of it, so that at the moment of its actualization it would also become, in its totality, a commonplace. Bad money drives out good. Non-novelty, as soon as it is put into circulation, drives out novelty, and does so in the most radical way, actualizing the non-existence of novelty simply by appearing, as non-novelty, in the field of poetry: '*calme bloc ici-bas* [ . . . ]'. And it is true, as these words by Mallarmé state in no uncertain terms, that, marked by such monuments, the field of poetry bears a strong resemblance to a graveyard.

We said: 'Some works of art have the *privilege*', but also: '*bad* money'. Our discourse shows an oscillation of values regarding the concept of commonplace, and such oscillation appears as a veritable semantic oscillation of the expression 'commonplace'. The same oscillation characterizes the presence of monuments in the graveyard of poetry: if on the one hand they warrant the objectification of the novelty par excellence in the *novissima*, the 'things of the ultimate end', and thus colour it with prophecy, on the other hand they move us to remember that *novissimi*, in Latin, can also mean the *rearguard*.

2. A very similar—in fact in some ways coinciding—oscillation characterizes the notion of the condition of childhood. Not only is there a symmetry between acknowledging childhood as endowed with autonomous values, a realm that is *other*, and poetry as a realm peopled with *other* inhabitants, but it is within one and the same process that these acknowledgements of *otherness* are achieved—subsequently leading to techniques of exploitation of the *others*. The *others* do not exercise power, but they do have *one* power available. The State of the *citoyens* has an interest in exploiting the power of which childhood is an inexhaustible reservoir, the forces childhood possesses autonomously, as its own prerogatives (the pedagogue exploits Émile to the advantage of the State), and that, for the State, guarantee the future in the very instant in which they come to characterize the rearguard. More hypocritical or shortsighted operations than Rousseau's will point to the *others* ('savage' children) as to a rearguard (where 'rear' carries the implication of *backward*

and hence a judgement of value) to be civilized— that is, exploited as a reservoir. Equally, those who exercise power are good at building monuments to the *others*. Erecting a monument to the poet works by collocating an *other* in a rearguard that is certainly backward—as a chronological judgement that translates into a relativized judgement of value—but sends forth some prophetic voices, *novissimae* forces. And the monument erected to the *other* by those who exercise power objectively tends to be identified with the *calme bloc ici-bas*, i.e. with the epiphany of what, in the creation of the *other*, tends to be posited as a monument. True, in the *calme bloc ici-bas* the tie between *novissima* and *novissimi* is as shown in the words from the *Oedipus at Colonus* quoted by Heidegger at the end of 'What Is Metaphysics?': 'For each thing the decision of the final fulfilment holds the event by its side'[1]—and therefore one will need very refined instruments to apprehend it by identification; but next to those who exercise power are also those who can fashion and use, 'according to intention', extremely refined instruments. If the State of the *citoyens* that is interested in childhood has Rousseau on its side, those who build monuments to *other* powers have Heidegger: I'm thinking especially of 'What Are Poets For?', where memory (*das Andenken*) gives the rhythm of the dialogue between the poet (an *other*) and the thinker—not a mediator between poet and non-poets, and yet a non-poet in dialogue with

---

1 Martin Heidegger, 'What Is Metaphysics?' (R.F.C. Hull and A. Crick trans) in *Existence and Being* (London: Vision Press, 1969), pp. 317–51. Translation modified to reflect as closely as possible Jesi's version of Heidegger's original: ('Überhallhin nämlich hält bei sich das Ereignete verwahrt ein Entscheid der Vollendung.'): Per ogni cosa la decisione del compimento finale tiene custodito presso di sé l'accaduto.' [Trans.]

the poet, just like Émile's pedagogue is not a mediator between child and adults and yet is a non-child who holds a dialogue with a child and, on behalf of the adults, exploits him.

3. At the end of September 1871, almost seventeen years old, Rimbaud leaves for Paris. 'On the eve of departure', Ernest Delahaye recalls, 'Rimbaud reads me the "Bateau ivre". "I've done this one," he says, "to show people in Paris".' There is no reason to doubt Delahaye's account, at least on this point: the 'Bateau ivre' was born under the sign of what connoisseurs of poetry by inspiration would judge as the original sin. It is almost a party piece: it was written 'to show people'. The very singular situation peculiar to Rimbaud, however, moves us to interpret this fact within two different frameworks—albeit parallel ones that at times coincide by transparency. On the one hand, it is the infantile situation of the child fearing the adult *others*, fearing his own exposure to them and precisely for that reason choosing that exposure, but doing so in what he—subjectively, and most often quite accurately—perceives as the manner most closely fitting the canon of the adults' enjoyment. On the other hand (but there is in fact a clear coincidence by transparency), if we configure Rimbaud as *other* by his being a *poet* rather than a child, the 'Bateau ivre' is merchandise on offer, something that can bring profit: and something meant to bring profit is necessarily made out of the matter of commonplaces. Not because the market always demands and pays for merchandise it already knows—far from it (and 'people in Paris' were in fact somewhat hard to please); rather, because the poet's tension towards the

successful placing of his merchandise is the attitude of openness par excellence to the commonplaces that fashion his creation into a thing. Not necessarily a known thing, but a thing nonetheless: not well known perhaps, and in fact brand new as to its presumed being in itself, but well known as to its being a thing, a piece of merchandise subject to appraisal. This is the route by which a work of art made out of the matter of commonplaces can enjoy the privilege of becoming itself a commonplace on the surface of the artist's creation. The 'Bateau ivre' was written 'to show people in Paris', but it is a thing, it is merchandise, objectively offered to posterity as well. The operation of opening oneself to reifying commonplaces, in which the poet and the child were jointly the *other*, thus translates into the monumental duration of the work on display, and through the transparent means of the grave-yard quality of the *calme bloc ici-bas*, shows how the strongest bond cementing the poet and the child consists of the close relationship they both have with death.

4. The child is not only closer to death than the adult, being closer to birth and hence to the threshold of non-existence. He is also, and more so than the adult, close to death because death can strike him more easily. For thousands of years (present times being a relative enough exception), the child, together with the old man or woman, was one about to die: the *enfant accroupi plein de tristesses* in the 'Bateau ivre' is joined with the old man in the 'Remembrances du vieillard idiot', which in fact consists of an evocation of childhood, or rather of the *jeunes crimes*. *Crimes, tristesses*: all signs of otherness and of commerce with death vis-à-vis the adults' realm—or

rather within its framework. To be an adult—neither *enfant accroupi* nor *vieillard idiot*—means exercising power, a long way from *crimes* and *tristesses*, a long way from death. Posterity is made of those who in some measure escape death indefinitely, and are therefore adults par excellence. They will have Rimbaud in their hands as the poet of the 'Bateau ivre', they will surely remark that 'the ending of the "Bateau ivre" prefigures Rimbaud's destiny',[2] and at the same time, almost horrified by the kind of merchandise they cannot help enjoying, will speak of the 'slender, fulgurating body of work that, at the end of the XIX century, Arthur Rimbaud left to us almost with disdain'. Thus, in a sort of catharsis, they will transfer onto the creator, confessing *through* the creator, the variously mitigated contempt that is always a peculiarity of the buyer towards the producer (where the producer has no other power than that intrinsic in producing): 'He produces—I alone can give value to his production by accepting it.' It is certainly true that Rimbaud 'hardly gave a thought to publishing anything' of what he wrote; but the 'Bateau ivre' was meant by him to have a use, to be exhibited, to literally be subjected to publication—albeit not through the printing press. The 'Bateau ivre' was written 'to show people': people, the adults, 'the powerful' (for adult poets, despite being poets, were identified with 'the powerful' in the eyes of

2 This and the following quotes are taken from the comment by Rolland de Renéville and Jules Mouquet to the 'Pléiade' edition of Arthur Rimbaud, *Œuvres complètes* (Paris: Gallimard, 1954). [All quotes from the English version of the poems are from Rimbaud, *Collected Poems* (Oliver Bernard trans.) (London: Penguin Classics 1986[1962]); translations modified.—Trans.]

the sixteen-year-old poet); and it was also objectively offered to the other category of the powerful that is made up by posterity, by the living par excellence, as adults are when compared to those who are about to die, whether *enfant accroupi* or *vieillard idiot*.

5. A commonplace, within our context, is a category of poetic matter exposed by the function of merchandise conferred by the poet upon one of his own works. What falls within this category is what makes the outcome of the creative operation into a thing. The 'Bateau ivre' is not only the actualizing of the commonplaces in Rimbaud's poetry, but an illustrated paradigm of the situation and process of this actualization. In it one can find the commonplaces (in our sense) that make a thing out of poetry written 'to show people'; but also the commonplaces (in the traditional meaning of the expression: the *topoi*) in Rimbaud's poetic writing, in turn interwoven with *Magasin Pittoresque*[3] commonplaces (*topoi*). Some *topoi* characteristic of Rimbaud's writing are images pertaining to the misery of childhood:

> *plus sourd que les cerveaux d'enfants*
> *un enfant accroupi plein de tristesses;* [4]

to religious themes:

---

3 In Douai, in September–October 1870, Rimbaud leafed through some issues of the *Magasin Pittoresque*; see E. de Rougemont, H. de Bouillane de Lacoste and P. Izambard, 'Recherche sur les sources du "Bateau ivre" et de quelques autres poèmes de Rimbaud', *Mercure de France* (15 August 1935).

4 'more absorbed than the minds of children / a child squatting full of sorrows'.

> *les pieds lumineux des Maries*
> *ainsi qu'une femme à genoux;*[5]

to erotica:

> *les rousseurs amères de l'amour*
> *baiser montant aux yeux [ . . . ] avec lenteurs.*[6]

*Magasin Pittoresque topoi* include all those related to the 'Poème de la Mer' and the 'incroyables Florides'.

Publication (in the literal sense), and hence the exhibition of peculiar *topoi* interwoven with *Magasin Pittoresque topoi*, is the process through which Rimbaud opened himself to commonplaces. The marketing of his work implicit in this choice also shows a *crime de jeunesse* consisting in the exhibition of one's own intimacy. One consequence of this exhibition, though, is access to the hypostases of reality—the commonplaces (not the *topoi*)— furnishing the pedagogic space in which adults force the child to live. After accessing death, the dead child in Rilke's second 'Requiem' discovers the futility of having learnt the names of things: this useless toil, masked as a recognition of the objective real, is forced onto each child, each and every *other*, in the realm of adults and of the 'civilized'. When the *other* is at the same time a child and a poet (or at least: when the operation of opening oneself to commonplaces can be ascribed to the child and at the same time to the poet), adjusting to this pedagogy is exhibition and marketing, accepting to be subjected to such pedagogy is driven by the need to survive and the need to profit from the work. The adults enforcing such pedagogy take on the form of those who

---

5 'the luminous feet of the Marys / like a woman on her knees'.
6 the bitter blushings of love / the kiss rising slowly to the eyes [...]'.

bestow profit and survival. The commonplaces called forth by that opening and flowing into it are circumscribed by significations appearing to be second in the order of perception, and thus still easily perceived: the identification with a thing, with the '*bateau*' winning freedom from mankind and attempting to experience a realm in which freedom is purification, clairvoyance and death:

> *L'eau verte pénétra ma coque de sapin*
> *Et des taches de vins bleus et des vomissures*
> *Me lava, dispersant gouvernail et grappin.*
> [ ... ]
> *Et j'ai vu quelquefois ce que l'homme a cru voir!*
> [ ... ]
> *Moi dont les Monitors et les voiliers des Hanses*
> *N'auraient pas repêché la carcasse ivre d'eau.*[7]

the symbols of the martyrdom implicit in the experience of that realm—the source of the nostalgia for the realm of non-freedom:

> *Mais, vrai, j'ai trop pleuré! Les Aubes sont navrantes.*
> [ ... ] *Je regrette l'Europe aux anciens parapets!*[8]

and finally the declaration of the incapability of not suffering, whether in one realm or the other:

> *Si je désire une eau d'Europe, c'est la flache*
> *Noire et froide* [ ... ]

---

7 'The green water penetrated my pinewood hull and washed me clean of the bluish wine-stains and the splashes of vomit, carrying away both rudder and anchor. [ ... ] And sometimes I have seen what men have imagined they saw! [ ... ] I, whose wreck, dead-drunk and sodden with water, neither Monitor nor Hanse ships would have fished up'.

8 'But, truly, I have wept too much! The Dawns are heartbreaking. [ ... ] I long for Europa with its age-old parapets!' (The second verse quoted here occurs first in the original poem.)

[ . . . ]
*Je ne puis plus, baigné de vos langueurs, ô lames,*
*Enlever leur sillage aux porteurs de cotons.*[9]

If, as is correct, we give only slight weight to Verlaine's remark ('the whole of the sea is in the "Bateau ivre"')— a flourish of banality that stops at what appear to be the primary significations in the poem—we have to admit that the 'second' significations probably were exactly the ones that 'people in Paris' might have liked best. And as we have said, these second significations stemmed from the joining of *topoi* peculiar to Rimbaud and *Magasin Pittoresque topoi*, formulations of existential novelty and current banalities, just as Rimbaud's life itself would be seen by posterity as the joining of a commonplace experience par excellence—leaving Europe—to a peculiarity specific to Rimbaud: leaving Europe, and not as a man of letters.

6. Although the opening out to commonplaces, the marketing of the work and the exhibition of intimacy are signs of an adjustment to the false objectivity imposed by adults, the reader of the 'Bateau ivre' will soon notice— when facing what we have called the second significations—that the commonplaces constitute an apparent ideological negation of the authoritarian premises of that false objectivity. The group of adults to whom Rimbaud had destined his 'Bateau ivre', the 'people in Paris', were themselves poets. Rimbaud mocked and

9 'If there is one water in Europe I want, it is the black cold pool [ . . . ] I can no more, bathed in your languors, O waves, sail in the wake of the carriers of cottons'.

despised the 'bourgeois' of Charleville. He mocked and despised the small town of Charleville. To Charleville and its inhabitants, he would oppose the mirage of Paris and 'people in Paris', remaining childishly far from an apprehension of the Internationale of adults and the ubiquity of its rule. He had chosen his own rulers among adults, and created within their realm a privileged *haut-lieu*. Yes, those rulers, in that *haut-lieu*, would also enjoy some commonplaces—but these would be presented as the opposite of the commonplaces enjoyed by adults in general and holding currency in their realm (though not in the *haut-lieu*). In the *haut-lieu*, one practised clairvoyance—the opposite of looking.

This insurrection relying on the succour of rulers nominated by mirage is articulated in what we might call the third order of signification in the 'Bateau ivre'. The two essential ganglia in these 'third' regions, in the apparent order of perception, are the human sacrifice determining the drunkenness-liberation of the *bateau*:

> *Je ne me sentis plus guidé par les haleurs*:
> *Des Peaux-Rouges criards les avaient*
>     *pris pour cibles,*
> *Les ayant cloués nus aux poteaux de couleurs*[10]

and the shrinking that is the ultimate mirage of the thing, the *bateau*, incapable of avoiding suffering whether in the realm of freedom or in that of non-freedom:

> *Si je désire une eau d'Europe, c'est la flache*
> *Noire et froide où vers le crépuscule embaumé*

---

10 'I no longer felt myself steered by the haulers: gaudy Redskins had taken them for targets, nailing them naked to coloured stakes'.

> *Un enfant accroupi plein de tristesses, lâche*
> *Un bateau frêle comme un papillon de mai.*[11]

The 'third' signification to which these two themes seem to point is in fact one. Both the human sacrifice and the metamorphosis of the *bateau* into a small paper boat declare a privilege of the condition of childhood: the *bateau* really is both the thing-child attaining freedom through the human sacrifice in which—at the hands of some *others*—the adults lose their lives, and the child's-thing, the small and fragile subject of the authority of a ruler who is also small and *plein de tristesses*: *un enfant accroupi*.

7. Rimbaud's participation in the fighting of the Commune is probably a legend. He was however a singular protagonist of that revolt—a *revolt* more than a *revolution*—in the guise of a prophet. He could only ever be the prophet of a revolt, not a revolution. The insurrection articulated in the actual simultaneity of the three layers of signification in the 'Bateau ivre' (apparently arrayed in order of perception) is tactically based on a sacrifice (marketing, exhibition) that is ransomed and made necessary by the mirage of the existence of clairvoyant and succouring rulers, of 'validators': adults, but only insofar as endowed with power—*bons poètes*. The opening to the common-places is a merely formal adhesion to the false objectivity of adults, of those who exercise power: in actual fact, its purpose is to gather forces for the revolt. These forces

---

11 'If there is one water in Europe I want, it is the black cold pool where into the scented twilight a child squatting full of sadness launches a boat as fragile as a butterfly in May'.

are weighed down by the crust of sin deriving from their being validated by adults; but the existence of mirage adults, clairvoyant rulers giving succour against other adults, ransoms them and makes them desirable, fit to be gathered in view of the revolt.

The word *revolution* correctly defines the complex of long- and short-term actions performed by those who are conscious of wanting to change a social, political and economical situation *within historical time*, and who elaborate tactical and strategic plans while constantly assessing relationships of cause and effect within historical time, taking the longest possible view. Every *revolt* can on the other hand be described as a suspension of historical time. The majority of those who take part in a revolt choose to engage their individuality in an action whose consequences they cannot either know or predict. At the moment of the clash, only a very small minority is conscious of the entire strategic plan (assuming there is one) within which the clash itself is positioned, as of a precise, albeit hypothetical, chain of cause and effect. In the clash of revolt the symbolic components of the ideology that put the strategy in motion are distilled, and they alone are really perceived by the insurgents. The opponent of the moment really becomes *the enemy*, the gun or stick really becomes *the weapon*, the victory of the moment really becomes *a good and righteous action* in defence of freedom and for the hegemony of one's class. Each revolt is a battle one has deliberately chosen to join. The instant of revolt determines the lightning-quick actualization and objectification of the self as part of a collectivity. The battle between good and evil, between survival and death, between success and failure, between adults and *others*, in which each and everyone is individually engaged on a daily basis, is identified with the battle of the entire collectivity: everyone has the same weapons, everyone is faced with the same obstacles, the one enemy, the *same enemy as ever*. Everyone experiences the epiphany of the same symbols: each person's individual space, dominated by personal symbols, the refuge from historical time that each finds in an individual symbology and mythology, widens into the symbolic space common to an entire collectivity, the refuge from historical time in which an entire collectivity finds an escape.

8. Each revolt is circumscribed by precise boundaries in historical space and historical time. Stretching before and after it are no man's land and the span of each person's life—the terrains on which ceaseless individual battles are fought. The concept of permanent revolution reveals—rather than an uninterrupted duration of revolt within historical time—the will to possess the ability to suspend historical time at any given moment so as to find a collective refuge in the symbolic space and time of revolt.

Up to the split second before the clash or the programmed action sparking the revolt, the potential insurgent is living, often with family, in his house or shelter; and although that residence and that environment may be provisional, precarious, conditioned by the imminent revolt, until the revolt begins they are the place of a more or less solitary individual battle that continues unchanged as in the days before the impending revolt: the individual battle between good and evil, between survival and death, between success and failure, between adults and *others*.

The sleep before the revolt—assuming the revolt will start at daybreak!—may well be as serene as that of the Prince of Condé, but lacks the paradoxical quiet of the moment of the clash.

We can love a city, recognize its streets and houses in our deepest secret memories; but only in the hour of revolt is a city truly felt as the *haut-lieu* and at the same time as *our* city: ours, because it belongs to the 'I' and at the same time to 'others'; ours, because it is the field of a battle chosen both individually and collectively; ours, because it is a circumscribed space where historical time is suspended and each act has a value of itself, in its absolutely immediate consequences. We take possession of a city by fleeing or advancing in the clash much more fully than by playing in its courtyards as children or strolling through its streets years later with a lover. In the hour of revolt we are no longer alone in the city; but when the revolt has passed, no matter its outcome, each of us reverts to being an individual in a society, whether better, worse or the same as before. When the clash has ended— one might be in jail, or in hiding, or in peace and quiet at home—the individual daily battles will resume. If historical time is not further suspended, in circumstances and for reasons that might well not be the same as those of the revolt, we revert to assessing each event and action on the basis of its certain or presumed consequences. The revolt had coincided with the sudden flash of an unusual quality of time, in which everything that happened, with extreme speed, seemed to be happening for ever. It was no longer a matter of living and acting within the framework of tactics and strategy, where medium-term objectives might be very far from the final objective while still prefiguring it—the greater the distance, the more anxious the wait. 'Now or never!' It was a matter of acting once and for all, and the fruit of the action was contained in the action itself. Each decisive choice, each irrevocable action, meant being in accord with time; any hesitation meant being outside time. When everything ended, some of the real protagonists had left the scene for ever.

9. The privilege of the condition of childhood is the tactical premise of Rimbaud's revolt. We are using the word 'privilege' in this case as well, since the condition of childhood in the 'Bateau ivre' is capable of enjoying vision and, above all, it is the condition by which vision is articulated. The poem is locked between two mirages: the sacrifice of the adults killed by the Redskins on the one hand; and the unwitting smallness and vulnerability of a tiny, fragile object in the hands of a child on the other. Both are mirages of non-responsibility: in the initial one, the thing-child has the vision of the non-responsibility acquired through the adults' sacrificial death; in the final one, the child's thing, like a child itself, has the vision of a realm of child rulers and child subjects, the *enfant accroupi* and the *bateau frêle*—and hence of a realm in which responsibility is shrunk to the measure of child's play, and fragility by excess is an objective deliverance from responsibility, within the framework of a nature concealing Europe, the *anciens parapets*, and adults. If the nature of the *incroyables Florides* is foreign to adults (and precisely for that reason is *incroyable*), the nature of Europe is almost an external projection of adults. For the *enfant accroupi*, both the *flache noire et froide* and the

*crépuscule embaumé* are ambivalent external projections of the super-realm governed by adults as a framework providing a horizon to his realm.

10. The initial mirage is a suspension of historical time by way of a human sacrifice; the final mirage is a suspension of historical time by way of a shrinking. Both are mirages of revolt, prophecies of a revolt of the *others*: 'In the air, high up, a long way off, a white, wild screaming'.[12] The word 'privilege' has so far joined within our discourse works of art that are made out of the matter of commonplaces (while being commonplaces on the surface of the artist's creations) with the condition of childhood, which in the 'Bateau ivre' is the condition allowing vision, and above all the condition by which vision is articulated. The relationship thus instated between commonplace and childhood works as a prelude to the recognition of an objective affinity between the 'commonplace condition' and the condition of childhood. The former is the condition of the artist acting to turn his creation into merchandise, a thing to be used, a thing that can be profitable, and in so doing opening himself to commonplaces, which at times flow into that opening and give matter to the work. The latter is the condition of the thing-child who acts from inside his own thingness and thus loves his being non-responsible and opens himself to a double vision: the vision of the killing of the adults resulting in his non-responsibility, and the vision of his being a child's thing, a non-responsible thing in the hands of a ruler-

---

12 Penultimate stage direction in Brecht's *Trommeln in der Nacht* (1919). [In English, see *Drums in the Night* (John Willett and Ralph Mannheim eds., John Willett trans.) (London: Methuen, 1980).—Trans.]

child, a *bateau frêle*. This objective affinity is the basis of Rimbaud's prophecy of revolt, as opposed to the adults' false pedagogic objectivity and to the false objectivity in the exploitation of those who produce merchandise. In those years the prophecy found occasion to confirm the maxim: 'What was promised will come to pass.' True, the reality of the Commune within historical space and time is far from Rimbaud's experience. Yet Rimbaud's life after 1873, and after his prophetic displacement of the revolt, seems to correspond to the paradigm of revolt, whether yesterday's or today's: when everything ended, some of the real protagonists had left the scene, for ever.

11. Having written that the poet has opened himself to commonplaces and that they have come, it seems legitimate to ask in what measure and in which way commonplaces (in our sense) might be endowed with objectivity. So far we have considered them as real entities, as things that come into the artist's creative experience and take possession of it. Where do they come from? And, first and foremost: are any of the possible answers to these questions destined to be adequate only within the scope of Rimbaud's poetry or his poetics, or are they also valid beyond it— do they move from a hypothetically wider scope, and do they remain significant within its supposedly greater width?

> *J'aimais les peintures idiotes, dessus de portes, décors, toiles de saltimbanques, enseignes, enluminures populaires; la littérature démodée, latin d'église, livres érotiques sans orthographe, romans*

*de nos aïeules, contes de fées, petits livres de l'enfance, opéras vieux, refrains niais, rythmes naïfs.*[13]

Certainly this is how Rimbaud spoke of commonplaces: those listed above (from 'Une saison en enfer') are the same as essentially coincide with those of our definition—poetic matter exposed by the function of merchandise that the poet confers upon the work. They are all merchandise: goods that reveal themselves as such *a posteriori*, outside the moment in which they were put to use, and that precisely through being dequalified and disused can serve as ingredients for the 'Alchimie du verbe'.[14] The 'Bateau ivre' itself is made out of the matter of this devalued merchandise, now retrieved by the poet through an alchemical operation in which it can once again be put to use as good merchandise. *Ce fut d'abord une étude. J'écrivais des silences, des nuits, je notais l'inexprimable. Je fixais des vertiges.*[15] But are these really the commonplaces that essentially coincide with those we have defined? What do we know of the *essence* of the former and the latter? Like myths, they are first and foremost something that a creative experience presses us to believe exists, while at the same time keeping its essence well concealed from us. Is it then legitimate to say that they *are*, they *come*, they *take possession*? So as to display

13 'I loved absurd pictures, fanlights, stage sceneries, mountebanks' backcloths, inn-signs, cheap coloured prints; unfashionable literature, church Latin, pornographic books badly spelt, grandmothers' novels, fairy stories, little books for children, old operas, empty refrains, simple rhythms'.
14  The title of the section of 'Une saison en enfer' from which the previous quote is taken.
15 'At first this was a study. I wrote silences and nights, expressed the inexpressible. I captured vertigos.'

their existence to us, Rimbaud defines for us (*j'aimais*) the forms and shapes meant to enclose them and to coincide with their essence to the point of translating it into an external surface. *J'aimais*, he says in 'Une saison en enfer'; and another *j'aimais* is implicit, and much reiterated, in the first person imperfect or past tense verbs in the 'Bateau ivre': *j'étais, j'ai vu, j'ai rêvé, j'ai suivi, j'ai heurté* . . . There is a veritable mythological machine at work here, *the* mythological machine, producing mythologies and pressing us to believe that the machine itself conceals myth within its impenetrable walls. If commonplaces are endowed with objective, autonomous essence and existence, then they come from an 'other world', for that is the only way we can denote a world that is not ours while being inhabited by them side by side with us, autonomously from us, without in any way interacting with us: in order to touch us, they have to *come*. To believe this is tantamount to believing that myth exists autonomously inside the mythological machine, which is situated—as the machine itself would have us believe— at the boundary between the two worlds. The parallel between these two acts of faith is such as to induce us to surmise something more than an equivalence: an essential coincidence by which a selfsame 'other world' appears in this world, cutting through history and suspending it, so that its epiphany takes on the alternately authentic guises of commonplace or mythologeme. To disbelieve this is equivalent to disbelieving the autonomous existence of myth inside the mythological machine; it is equivalent to being convinced that the mythological machine is in fact empty (or full of nothing but itself, which is the same), and that myth, like the essence of the commonplaces that can be put to use in the 'Alchimie du verbe', is solely a void to which the mythological machine refers—the essence of commonplaces, a void to which the 'Alchimie du verbe' in turn refers. In this case as well, the coincidence is especially significant: both mythological machine and 'Alchimie du verbe' appear to be presumable aspects of the selfsame functioning complex, of the same machine, whose first function is to refer to the void of being.

12. At this point we seem to be coming up against a polarity: faith vs non-faith. Yet, at least within the limits of our language (the limits, that is, within which the word 'polarity' has meaning), such polarity is in fact not there. To believe that myth autonomously resides inside the mythological machine—that the essence of the commonplace autonomously resides in the 'Alchimie du verbe'— can only mean that myth *is not there*—that the essence of the commonplace *is not*. If they are there, they are in an 'other world': they *not-are there*. (*J'écrivais des silences* [ . . . ] *je notais l'inexprimable. Je fixais des vertiges*). Even the most strenuous supporter of non-faith is forced to consent to an involuntary act of faith: there is no more exact faith in an 'other world' that *not-is there* than the declaration that such 'other world' is not. The word 'there' strictly adheres to Rimbaud's *j'aimais* and only indicates deliberate vs involuntary adhesion.

There is in fact an important difference between negating in order to affirm and negating in order to deny, between saying that the 'other world' *not-is there* and saying that it *is not*. While of absolutely no use as to instructing us about that world, since our language remains inert before the mirage of becoming 'the arrow [that] survives the string, so that gathered in leaping, it may be *more* than itself',[16] this difference is very instructive about the behaviour of those between which it discriminates. Those in the '*there not-is*' camp can belong to the revolt and are certainly predisposed to become its prophets, to be used as its prophets or supporters promising its repeatability; those in the '*is not*' camp have in front of them only the revolution—or conservatism, if they decide to give up on themselves and accept the relationships of forces in which they find themselves. The allure of revolt rests first and foremost on its immediate inevitability: it must ineluctably happen. Time is suspended: what is, *is* once and for all. As in alchemy, if the experiment fails, it is because one had not been pure and conscious enough. There will be another, a thousand other suspensions of time, and possibly, once, the sufficient purity and awareness will be achieved. The prophet announces the suspension of time, and also the repeatability of such suspensions. Revolution can be much less fascinating precisely because it is extremely hard and uncertain to establish what its correct timing might be, and also because, not being inevitable at the right time, if it does not take place at the right moment it might not come about again for an indefinitely long time.

13. Neither one nor the other (neither revolt nor revolution) contradicts on a conceptual level the model proposed

---

16 Rainer Maria Rilke, *Duineser Elegien*, I, vv. 52–3 (Leipzig: Insel Verlag, 1923). [English translation: *Duino Elegies*, Bilingual EDN (David Oswald trans.) (Switzerland: Daimon Verlag, 1997); translation modified.—Trans.]

by the mythological machine. Far from it: in the perspective opened by either, this model ends up being identified with the *a priori* that stands as the solid and obscure foundation of the gnoseological process. Faced with the essence of the commonplace—or the essence of myth—one has no authentic conceptual alternative but only an alternative based on gesture, on behaviour—behaviour that remains in any case circumscribed within the box delimited by the walls of the mythological machine. On a conceptual level, both revolt and revolution remain nothing but different articulations (suspension of time vs 'right' time) of the time obtaining within that box. The 'drunken boat' did not sever that time, but merely enjoyed its limited suspension—which, crucially, was not brought about by the 'boat', but arrived as an epiphany so that the latter could enjoy it: *Je ne me sentis plus* [ . . . ]. Nor would time have been severed if, instead of a revolt, a revolution had happened (if the 'boat', having calculated the most opportune moment, the 'right' moment, had done away with its sailors like a menacing *Potëmkin* intolerant not only of its officers but of all men): time would have been privileged, declared 'right', but not severed, for faced with the root of time, with the void of being that is found inside the mythological machine and referred to by it, revolution would have declared an 'is not' that perfectly coincides with the ontological argument.

In the 'Bateau ivre', failure to experience the realm of freedom in terms of poetic matter paves the way for Rimbaud's critique of the privilege of poetic matter which will lead to his forsaking creative work and to his Abyssinian experience: from the commonplace in the locus of poetry to the commonplace in the locus of gesture and behaviour. If Rimbaud's poetic activity constitutes a moment of revolt, his activities as a trader and traveller in Africa constitute a moment of revolution. It is however a solitary, pessimistic revolution, stemming from the belief that it is impossible to sever time and, above all, the root of time, the void of being that we may call 'myth' or 'the essence of commonplaces'. Severing this root would mean having available a language or a set of gestures such as could oppose the mythological machine on a plane that would enable one to declare at the same time the existence and non-existence of what the machine purports to contain: *J'écrivais des silences* [ . . . ] *je notais l'inexprimable*. It is precisely in the pessimistic quality and in the solitary, individual character of this revolution that the childlike component of the second part of Rimbaud's life is shipwrecked after the forsaking of poetry. Yes, the forsaking of Europe is a commonplace compatible with childhood: but choosing to forsake Europe when one no longer believes in the liberating effectiveness of doing so means renouncing the condition of childhood and becoming part of the realm of adults— the only people who accept to devote themselves to revolutions whose failure, from the outset, they take for granted. If the 'Bateau ivre' was written 'to show people', the second part of Rimbaud's life was also lived as merchandise, so that the realm of adults would see Arthur Rimbaud grown into an adult.

# Knowability of the Festival

EDITOR'S NOTE

In the spring of 1972, Jesi began the 'very complicated work on the origin of the mythological fact' that would keep him busy for quite a while and would result in the elaboration of the 'mythological machine model'. At the same time he was planning to publish *La festa. Antropologia, etnologia, folklore*,[1] the anthology that with his many other writing commitments would engage him for several years (it was completed in June 1976, and would be published exactly one year later). The introduction to *La festa* is the masterpiece titled 'Knowability of the Festival', Jesi's last great essay on the 'machine' and its several articulations.

On the one hand, Jesi unfolds in this essay an investigation that 'might adequately and paradoxically be called "Unknowability of the Festival"', analysing the current impossibility that stops us making contact with genuine myth or with an authentic festive experience, and studying the modalities of 'non-knowledge' of the festival, that is, the modalities and occasions by which the machine functions.

On the other hand, after his reckoning with the 'commonplace' (to which he prefers, both here and in the interview that closes this book, Bachofen's concept of a 'symbol resting upon itself'), he employs a technique of *knowledge by composition* in which 'using', 'studying', 'quoting', 'putting to work' are perfectly synonymous and coincide with the expression in Benjamin's *Theses on the Philosophy of History*: '[T]o seize hold of a memory as it flashes up at the moment of danger'. Thus

---

1 Furio Jesi, *La festa. Antropologia, etnologia, folklore* (Turin: Rosenberg & Sellier, 1977). [Trans.]

beyond the 'situation that makes machines real and productive', what remains is the utopian and 'exclusively political' chance to take possession of the myth-memory. In the final, astonishing pages of this essay, Jesi sets out, as he wrote in another letter to Giulio Schiavoni, the possibility of 'conquering the past as a prophecy of the future—a future that is not predictable on the basis of the past'.

In a few parenthetic references, but also in his notes, Jesi recalls the Epilogue, the Materials (i.e. the essays by Kerényi, Arnold van Gennep, Josef Haeckel and others) and the Appendices to *La festa*.

The Appendices quoted are: (i) 'From Letter X of Part 4 of *La Nouvelle Héloïse* (1761) by Jean-Jacques Rousseau'; (ii) 'How to Honour Christian Festivals' from Giuseppe Capecelatro, *Le feste de' Cristiani* (1771); (iii) 'The Feast of Fools and Subdeacons' from Jacques-Antoine Dulaure, *Histoire abrégée de différens cultes* (1805); (iv) 'Festivals of the French Revolution' from Adolphe Thiers, *Histoire de la Révolution française*, VOL. 5 (1823–27).

The Materials quoted are: (2) 'Festivals of the Natives' from André Thevet, *Cosmographie universelle, illustrée de diverses figures des choses plus remarquables veuës par l'auteur* (1575), (3) 'Festivals of the American Savages', from Père Joseph-François Lafitau, *Mœurs des sauvages amériquains, comparées aux mœurs des premiers temps* (1724) and (4) 'The "tsantsa" Festival of the Jibaro' from Sigfrid Rafael Karsten, *Blood Revenge, War and Victory Feasts Among the Jibaro Indians of Eastern Ecuador* (1923).

# Knowability of the Festival

## 1. LITERATURE: CRUEL FESTIVAL AND INNER FESTIVAL

In *La letteratura della Nuova Italia*,[1] Croce recalls his exasperation when in 1906, 'as the Vesuvius eruption was raging at its worst [ . . . ], when the streets of Naples were choked with heaps of heavy yellow-brown ash', he received 'as if that wrath of God were nothing at all' an issue of *Il Marzocco*[2] with an article by Angelo Conti bearing 'a rapturous, awestruck title: "The Festival of Fire".' Conti wrote about the volcano erupting:

> It is not possible to imagine anything more awful or grandiose. Here, in the land of the sun and the sirens, earth has celebrated her festival of fire. Man has been excluded, pushed out, deranged with horror and terror [ . . . ]

and recalled the passage from the *Germania* in which Tacitus speaks of the festival with its 'frightful chariot [ . . . ] bearing a simulacrum of Herta across a wood to the shore of a

---

1 Benedetto Croce, *La letteratura della Nuova Italia. Saggi critici* (*Scritti di storia letteraria e politica*, 33) (Bari: Laterza,1957), VOL. 6, 190ff. All subsequent quotations from Croce and Angelo Conti are from the same source.

2 A weekly literary review based in Florence, published between 1896 and 1932. [Trans.]

lake',[3] her 'men consecrated to death accompanying the deity under sinister shadows'. And that was not all. Conti was truly overcome by the urge to enclose Naples, the Vesuvius, the 'sun and the sirens' and the saints within the sphere of his 'festival'. 'Even San Gennaro,' Croce remarked, 'a saint well known and familiar in his old guise to us Neapolitans, among whom Conti was living at the time, was refashioned for us as his "Dionysian Saint".' A devotee of a trinity that included the simulacra, if not the authentic effigies, of Nietzsche, Ruskin and D'Annunzio, Conti recognized in the 'festival'—his 'festival of fire'—a singular epiphany of all that is ancient, and thus also of what is Dionysian; and with the audacity of an 'aphilological'[4] comparatist or maker of combined forms, took the liberty of clothing San Gennaro in a few scraps from *Die Geburt der Tragödie*:[5]

> He was quickened by the spirit of fire, as if he had been born of the ardent, exterminating mountain. So much so that, ever since the day of his death under Diocletian, his blood still boils, as if made of the same matter that seethes in the womb of volcanoes.

'And so on and so forth', Croce concludes; while however taking the occasion, precisely as he recalls his indignation against 'The Festival of Fire', to oppose

---

3 See Tacitus, *The Agricola and the Germania* (James Rives ed., Joun Mattinlgy introd. and trans.) (London: penguin Classics, 2010). [Trans.]

4 An adjective used by Croce to condemn Bachofen: see Benedetto Croce, 'Il Bachofen e la storiografia afilologica', *Atti della Reale Accademia di scienze morali e politiche di Napoli* 51(1928): 1.

5 Friedrich Nietzsche, *The Birth of Tragedy & Other Writings* (Ronald Speirs trans.) (Cambridge: Cambridge University Press 1999). [Trans.]

Conti's 'allegorical excogitations' by evoking the tragedy of 1906 in an exquisitely literary page of his own: a page that has the outspoken purpose of serving as an authentic witness account of the facts, as against their specious, 'aestheticizing' use:

> [W]ith the Vesuvian eruption of spring 1906 raging at its worst, when the streets of Naples were choked with heaps of heavy yellow-brown ash, and passers-by disfigured by that dust, when roofs needed to be constantly and rapidly cleared, lest they collapse, of the weight that relentlessly fell on them, and a huge black globe of ash sailed over the gulf threatening to break open over the city, and all was dark and sombre, and the populace was already beginning its frightening chanting processions.

A page—this one by Croce—undoubtedly more refined than Conti's; but whether through intention (to show by comparison how one should in fact 'write well' about the eruption, with no 'display of image-making combinations'), or through the spontaneity devoid of— or autonomous from—immediate objectives of Croce's style, a page which nonetheless also saw in the 'memories of history' the discovery and evocation of a 'festival'.

Of a cruel 'festival', certainly; of a 'festival' absolutely devoid of allegorical implications or metaphysical symbolism; of a 'festival' that, unlike the earthquake of Lisbon in Voltaire's evocation[6] or—if we wish to abound

---

6 Voltaire, *Poème sur le désastre de Lisbonne* (1756) / 'The Lisbon Earthquake' in *Candide; or Optimism* (Tobias Smollett trans.) (London: Penguin Books, 2005), p. 107]. [Trans.]

in comparisons by denial and neglect measure and artistic perspective—the plague of Athens in the *De rerum natura*,[7] did not lead to any considerations on the human condition or the relationship between man and nature. An evocation of a 'festival' nonetheless, if we choose to give the word *festival* the meaning it has come to acquire within the scope of the human sciences, or rather the meaning deriving from a historical consideration of its connotations within that scope.[8]

---

7 See Lucretius, *On the Nature of Things* (M. F. Smith trans.) (Indianapolis: Hackett, 2001). [Trans.]

8 We shall also, however, have to take into account some of the main contributions to the study of the festival in classical times: Ernst Samter, *Familienfeste der Griechen und Römer* (Berlin: Reimer, 1901); Martin P. Nilsson, *Griechische Feste* (Leipzig: Teubner, 1906); Ludwig Deubner, *Attische Feste* (Berlin: Keller, 1932); Martin P. Nilsson, *Die Entstehung und religiöse Bedeutung des griechischen Kalenders*, (Lund: C.W.K. Gleerup, 1962); Giulia Piccaluga, *Elementi spettacolari nei rituali festivi romani*, (Rome: Edizioni dell'Ateneo, 1965); also William Warde Fowler, *The Roman Festivals* (London: Macmillan, 1925). Although in [*La festa*] we have not examined the problem of Greek and Roman festivals, we have often drawn on the available academic publications on the subject for the Introduction and Epilogue [to that volume]. For some elements of the notion of 'festival', we have also used works of an essentially descriptive and documentary character, such as: Heino Pfannenschmid, 'Germanische Erntfeste in heidn. u. christl. Cultus, mit bes. Beziehung a. Niedersachsen' in *Beitr. z. german. Altertumskunde u. kirchl. Archäologie*, 1878; Angelo De Gubernatis, *Storia comparata degli usi nataliʒi in Italia e presso gli altri popoli indoeuropei* (Milan: Treves, 1878; Bologna: Forni, 1969. Anastatic reprint) and *Storia comparata degli usi nuʒiali in Italia e presso gli altri popoli indoeuropei* (Milan: Treves, 1878; Bologna: Forni, 1969. Anastatic reprint), to which it is still useful to compare the works of Hermann Usener, *Das Weihnachtsfest* (1889) and *Christliche Festbräuche* (1889); Vincenzo Forcella, 'Tornei e giostre, ingressi trionfali e feste carnevalesche' in *Roma sotto Paolo III* (Rome: T. Artigianelli, 1885); and, more recently, the studies collected by Jean Jacquot in the two volumes of *Les fêtes de la Renaissance* and *Fêtes et cérémonies au temps de Charles Quint* (Paris: CNRS, 1959–60); Friedrich Sieber, *Volk und volkstümliche Motivik im Festwerk des Barocks*, (Berlin: Akademie-Verlag,

The fate of the festival in our modern society and culture may be preliminarily described in these words by Kerényi:

> [S]uch acts can *only* be performed in a festive manner: only on a plane of human existence that is different from the quotidian. Tradition merely replaces one's intimate need to attain that plane; but if it must also replace festivity, then the entire festival acquires something dead, grotesque even, like the movements of dancers for those who have gone deaf and can no longer hear music. And those who cannot hear music cannot dance: without festive feeling there is no festival.[9]

This was how Kerényi stressed the main traits of our relationship with the festival: both with the festival as we observe it (hence with the festival of those seen as other, of the *others*), and with the mirages of festivals *of our own* to which at times we seek to adapt our gestures and states of mind so as to be protagonists, rather than mere observers, of a festive situation. With regard to the festivals of the *others* we find ourselves exactly in the situation of those who observe the dancers' movements but have 'gone deaf and can no longer hear music'. As for our attempts to adapt to mirages of a festival *of our own*—almost as if such mirages were latencies to be actualized—they can only lead to 'something dead,

---

1960); Paolo Toschi, *Invito al folklore italiano. Le regioni e le feste* (Rome: Studium, 1963).

9 Quoted from the Italian translation: Károly Kerényi, *La religione antica nelle sue linee fondamentali* (Delio Cantimori trans.) (Rome: Astrolabio, 1959), p. 48. [See *The Religion of the Greeks and Romans* (Christopher Holme trans.) (London: Thames and Hudson, 1962).]

grotesque even', resembling the performances of those
who might insist on dancing not only when they have
gone deaf but also in the objective absence of music. We
cannot in fact avail ourselves of any historical relationship (unless one of pure observation—partial and precarious at that—of the *others*) with 'festive feeling',
with 'the festive'. We are, above all, estranged from the
*collective* quality of a 'festive' sense such as would have
'in [its] innermost recesses [ . . . ] something closer to joy
than to melancholy'.[10] The only *sui generis* 'festival' that
remains accessible to us is the 'cruel festival'—showing,
it is true, a collective experience, but only one of violence
and grief. From this point of view, the plague of Athens
in *De rerum natura* was already a 'cruel festival', presented
as a prime example of collective experience belonging to
a time or, more precisely, to an evocative context (that
of Lucretius) which excluded *a priori* the possibility—
peculiar to the festival—of 'taking part [through it] in
the free play of the gods.'[11] Among the 'cruel festivals' of
this sort, sharing this common denominator beyond the
huge intrinsic differences between their respective contexts, are the Lisbon earthquake in Voltaire's evocation
and the plague in Milan (but also the insurrection of the
populace of Milan in which Renzo is caught up) in *The
Betrothed*.[12] Croce's indignation against Conti's 'Festival
of Fire', and at the same time his own taste for giving an
artistic image of the eruption (albeit an *a posteriori* one

---

10 Kerényi, *La religione antica*.

11 Kerényi, *La religione antica*, p. 60

12 Alessandro Manzoni's *I promessi sposi*, published in several versions
between 1827 and 1842. [See *The Betrothed: A Tale of XVII Century Milan*
(A. Colquhon trans.) (New York: Alfred A. Knopf, 2013)]. [Trans.]

created at the moment of re-evocation), are an occasional (if no less meaningful) sign of the need not only to refuse as rash and 'unserious' any attempt to transfigure a catastrophe into a mysterious festival of inhuman mirth through 'rapturous, awestruck' words, but also to counter it with the picture of the 'cruel festival'. A cruel festival devoid of any metaphysical implications, the simple collective human experience of a distressing time, and nonetheless a 'festival': a 'festival' in the negative, the empty mould of what the 'festival' once was. When the festival is no longer possible for want of the social and cultural premises of an experience of collectivity that is 'in its innermost recesses [ . . . ] closer to joy than to melancholy', the memory of the lost ancient festival becomes so starkly outlined in the light of nostalgia as to draw into the ambit of the negative 'festival', of the empty mould, any experience that is collective, sorrowful and in some measure corresponding—in the negative— to the features of the real festival.[13]

The very title of this essay, 'Knowability of the Festival', underscores *our* way of knowing the true festival. What we have been saying already points to the fact that a knowability of the festival is for us extremely problematic. Thus, saying that the present situation draws into the empty mould of the true festival any collective and sorrowful experience that may in any measure correspond—in the negative—to the features of the true festival means referring to those 'features of the true festival' that we are able to know—albeit in a precarious,

13 Furio Jesi, 'Cesare Pavese, dal mito della festa al rito del sacrificio' in *Letteratura e mito* (Turin: Einaudi, 2002[1968]), pp. 161–76.

problematic way. If in order to obtain a synthesis of such features we turn to a modern thinker such as R. Caillois, who has given particular attention to the question of the true festival, we find the following answer:

> This interval of universal confusion represented by the festival masquerades [ . . . ] as the moment in which the world order is abrogated. Therefore all excesses are allowed during it. Your behaviour must be contrary to the rules. Everything should be back to front. In the mythic age the course of time was reversed: one was born as an old man, and died a child [ . . . ]. In this way all those laws which protect the good natural and social order are systematically violated.[14]

This approach to the festival is effected by following an equivocal middle path between ethnographic observation and the exegesis of a society that is *other* but deemed to be legitimately workable as a cognitive model of our own. When analysed in detail, Caillois' arguments are found to be interspersed with information retrieved from the history of religion, the philosophy of religion, the science of folklore, and from ethnology or cultural anthropology, etc. 'Universal confusion', 'the world order [ . . . ] abrogated'—this is the purview of the history of religions: beyond these words are the materials relative to the periodical festivals of renewal of nature and its cosmic order, as mirrored in the elements of renewal of

---

14 Roger Caillois, 'Théorie de la fête', *La Nouvelle Revue Française* 316 (January 1940): 49, quoted in Max Horkheimer and Theodor W. Adorno, *Dialettica dell'illuminismo* (Lionello Vinci trans.) (Turin: Einaudi, 1966). [See *Dialectic of Enlightenment* (John Cumming trans.) (London: Verso Books, 1997), p. 105.]

social institutions which, not without precise philosophy of religion implications, M. Eliade chose as the foundation of *Mythe de l'éternel retour*.[15] 'Your behaviour must be contrary to the rules. Everything should be back to front': this is rather the purview of folklore and of medieval traditions which, recalling the 'world back to front', seem connected to folklore's 'Land of Cockaigne', to the 'Feast of Fools', etc.[16] 'One was born as an old man, and died a child'—the direct reference is to the practice of initiation, through which an adolescent (a 'child') would ritually die so as to be [re]born as an adult ('old').[17]

Already for Caillois, and more so even for Horkheimer and Adorno, who quoted him in *Dialektik der Aufklärung*,[18] these scattered limbs of scientific knowledge as applied to the festival can be organically gathered by the sociologist.

> In pleasure men disavow thought and escape civilization. In the ancient societies festivals offered a communal celebration of this reversion. The primitive orgies are the collective origin of enjoyment.[19]

---

15 Mircea Eliade, *Le mythe de l'éternel retour. Archétypes et répétition* (Paris: Gallimard, 1949) / *The Myth of the Eternal Return: Cosmos and History* (Willard Trask trans.) (Princeton: Princeton University Press, 2005).]

16 See Giuseppe Cocchiara, *Il paese di Cuccagna e altri studi di folklore* (Turin: Einaudi, 1956), pp. 159–87; also: Jesi, Appendix III to *La festa*.

17 C. J. Bleeker (ed.), 'Initiation. Contributions to the Theme of Study-Conference of the International Association for the History of Religions'. Strasbourg (17–22 September 1964) in 'Studies in the History of Religions', Supplements to *Numen* 10 (1965).

18 See note 13.

19 Horkheimer and Adorno, *Dialectic of Enlightenment*, p. 105.

The expression 'primitive orgies' rings somewhat false; or rather, uttered by Horkheimer and Adorno, it takes on the colours of pre-1914 Europe (that is, before the 'world festival of death'[20]): it is a sort of 'verb' evocative of the savages put on show by the Freud of *Totem und Tabu*[21] as they walked through the streets of Vienna and in front of whom the Musil of *Der Mann ohne Eigenschaften* would ironically take the stance of the positivist ethnographer, who first and foremost determines by barometer and thermometer the situation of his own work *in loco*:

> A barometric low hung over the Atlantic. It moved eastward toward a high pressure area over Russia without as yet showing any inclination to bypass this high in a northerly direction. The isotherms and isotheres were functioning as they should. The air temperature was appropriate to the annual mean temperature [ . . . ]. The water vapour in the air was at its maximal state of tension, while the humidity was minimal. In short, to put it in words that, albeit rather quaintly, perfectly describe the facts: it was a fine day in August 1913.[22]

---

20 This is the expression used by Thomas Mann in the last sentence of *Der Zauberberg* (1924): 'Wird auch aus diesem Weltfest des Todes, auch aus der schlimmen Fieberbrunst, die rings den regnerischen Abendhimmel entzündet, einmal die Liebe steigen?'

21 Sigmund Freud, '*Totem und Tabu*' in *Gesammelte Werke*, VOL. B.9 (London: Imago, 1940) / *Totem and Taboo: Resemblances Between the Psychic Lives of Savages and Neurotics* (A. A. Brill trans.) (Amherst, NY: Prometheus Books, 2000).[Trans.]

22 Robert Musil, *L'uomo senza qualità*, (Anita Rho trans.) (Turin: Einaudi, 1965), p. 5 / *The Man Without Qualities*, VOL. 1 (Burton Pike ed., Sophie Wilkins trans.) (New York: Vintage, 1996), p. 3 [translation modified.]

As against Caillois' positions, quoted in *Dialektik der Aufklärung*, that mention 'primitive orgies' and seem to minutely explain what a true festival might be, Musil's novel offers a model of 'impossible festival': the celebrations for the jubilee of Franz Josef, the 'Parallel Campaign', the wanting to dance at all costs even though the music is objectively over (and should it still be playing, we could not hear it anyway).

This theme of the 'impossible festival'—an impossibility that Caillois seems to at least want to counter with a knowability of the festival set out in scientific terms—recurs before Musil (albeit much more superficially) in the late nineteenth-century novel: 'There are no more beautiful festivals. We are too ugly, and everything has been seen too much already', as a character says in M. Prévost's *Demi-vierges*.[23] True, in *Le spleen de Paris*, Baudelaire had proclaimed the freshness of another authentic festival: 'O night! O refreshing darkness! You are for me the sign of an inner festival, you are the deliverance from anguish!'[24] But Baudelaire's 'festival' was precisely an 'inner' festival, and as such something much removed from the 'true festival' studied by ethnologists and sociologists ('inner', in Baudelaire's context, also stands for 'individual', whereas the 'true festival' of the *others* is first and foremost a collective experience). The inner festival is the only alternative to the cruel festival that can retain some freshness in the relationship between

---

23 Marcel Prévost, *Les Demi-vierges* (Aldo Mario trans.) (Milan: Baldini, Castoldi & C., 1906), p. 134.

24 Charles Baudelaire, 'Le crépuscule du soir' in *Œuvres complètes* (Y.-G. Le Dantec ed.) (Paris: Gallimard, 1954), p. 315 / *The Poems in Prose* (Francis Scarfe trans.) (Manchester: Carcanet, 2011), p. 99 [translation modified.]

modern man and 'the festive'. Pages such as the famous ones from *Tonio Kröger* show the point of coincidence between inner festival and cruel festival where they evoke festivals that are cruel for the individual as they draw him into a dimension of collective 'enjoyment' that is denied to him and that translates into a melancholic impulse towards the enjoyment (not devoid of pathos) of the inner festival:

> Instead he was looking into himself, where there was so much sorrow and so much burning desire. Why? Why was he there? Why was he not sitting at the window in his room, reading *Immensee* and looking out now and again at the garden wrapped in twilight, where the old walnut tree was creaking heavily? That would have been his place. Let others dance, let them dance with skill and fire![25]

Here on the other hand our discourse seems to be veering towards Proust, as the author par excellence of the 'festival' in the modern novel. The shift from *Tonio Kröger* to Proust is less arbitrary than it might seem, if we consider that 'festivals', while of course being part of what E. Wilson[26] defined as the Proustian 'social fresco', are—as points of special concentration—the places that

---

25 Thomas Mann, *Tonio Kröger* (Remo Costanzi trans.) (Milan: Rizzoli, 1954), p. 27–8 / *Tonio Kröger and Other Stories* (David Luke trans.) (New York: Bantam Books 1970) [translation modified]; and Theodor Storm, *Immensee and Other Stories* (Ronald Taylor, Bayard Quincy Morgan and Frieda M. Voigt trans) (Richmond: Alma Classics, 2015).]

26 Edmund Wilson, *Il castello di Axel. Studio degli sviluppi del simbolismo tra il 1870 e il 1930* (Marisa and Luciana Bulgheroni trans) (Milan: Il Saggiatore, 1965), p. 130 / *Axel's Castle: A Study in the Imaginative Literature of 1870–1930* (New York: Modern Library, 1996).

best reveal the radical internalization of Proust's narrative, the actual internalization of phenomena circumscribed in historical time (E. Canetti would speak of 'mastication', 'ingestion', 'incorporation'[27]). The festive gatherings recurring in Proust's *Recherche*[28] are cruel festivals, not so much because the cruelty of the age is manifested through them and around them, but because they are acted upon by the *narrator's* cruelty: because Proust has composed them as a gastronomic preparation offered to the cruel devouring god of art and ahistorical time whose regent he is—and the cruelty of the devouring god preliminarily bleeds its colour into the food, which he could not otherwise find palatable. Cruel festivals, and inner festivals as well: cruel because destined to be introjected, ingested. In Proust *as much as* in Mann, the cruelty of the festival is the fruit of the realization, and also the proof, of the impossibility of a true festival. In *Tonio Kröger* the apparent contraposition of the vitality of the festival to the 'death' of those who, like Tonio, are unable to take part in it without anguish, is ambiguously situated between tragic vision and ironical vision. The festive gatherings on the *Zauberberg* will then explicitly show what sickness was hiding behind that vitality and take on a starkly grotesque, demonic hue.[29] Similarly in Proust—not wanting to push too far into the (hardly existent)

---

27 Elias Canetti, *Massa e potere* (Furio Jesi trans.) (Milan: Rizzoli, 1972), pp. 219–28 / *Crowds and Power* (Carol Stewart trans.) (New York: Seabury Press, 1978).]

28 Marcel Proust, *À la recherche du temps perdu*, I–IV (Paris: Gallimard, 1989–2019) / *In Search of Lost Time* (Christopher Prendergast ed., Lydia Davis trans.) (London: Penguin, 2003).

29 See, in particular, the paragraph 'Walpurgisnacht' in Chapter 5, or the 'feast' decreed by Mynheer Peeperkorn in Chapter 7 ('Vingt et un').

Proust/Thomas Mann parallel—the contraposition between the historical time of the festive gatherings that are narrated and the ahistorical time of the narrator, and hence between the situation of the eaten vs that of the eater, is an implicit declaration of the impossibility of a collective and non-cruel festival. The Proustian contraposition reveals the identity between the narrator and the protagonists of festive gatherings taking place not in his own time but in the eighteenth century, and of which the gatherings contemporary to Proust were a late reflection. Eighteenth-century festive gatherings were already on the outer borders of the true festival. In distinguishing them from those that took place in the Renaissance and in the baroque age, J. Starobinski writes:

> If masks, incognito and disguise are still admissible, the important thing is not the play-acting but the moving while unseen, the spying, the being recognized while remaining hidden.[30]

Proust took these features to their extreme limit, translating his own relationship to festive gatherings within historical time into pure 'spying', 'being recognized while remaining hidden', which was the act preparing the introjection, the preliminary intervention to be operated on the food that would be ingested:

> As far as we know, even at the beginning of his public career he was so bizarre as to force Prince Antoine Bibesco and his brother to visit him

---

30 Jean Starobinski, *La scoperta della libertà. 1700–1789* (Manuela Busino-Maschietto trans.) (Milan: Fabbri Skira, 1965, p. 85; also Abscondita, 2008) / *The Invention of Liberty, 1700–1789* (Bernard C. Swift trans.) (Cleveland: Skira/World Publishing Company, 1964).

late at night and describe to him the festive gatherings in which he had not taken part.[31]

The festive gatherings that Proust at the same time organizes and spies upon (respectively in two different dimensions of his space, ahistory and history, later aligned as two phases—preparation and introjection—of the same operation) find their archetype in the untimely and joyful, if somewhat shrill, festival in Hoffmann's novella *The Heart of Stone*:

> Every three years, on the day of the Nativity of the Virgin, he would celebrate in his villa the festival of the good old time; he would invite anyone who might like to come from the city, but under the imperative condition that each guest should wear a costume dating back to the year 1760.[32]

Yet Proust's festive gatherings show a more explicit *facies hippocratica*, and this corresponds to the fact that (unlike Hoffmann), after organizing his 'festival of the good old time', Proust penetrates it like a spy *à la Kierkegaard*, for the purpose of taking possession of it—nor could he truly take possession of it if this were not something falsely alive, a dance in the absence of music.

## 2. SPIABILITY OF THE 'OTHER'

We have just observed a paradoxical situation. Convinced of the current impossibility of a collective festival that is

---

31 Wilson, *Il castello di Axel*, p. 153

32 E. T. A. Hoffmann, 'Il cuore di pietra' (1817) in *Romanzi e racconti*, VOL. 1 (Carlo Pinelli ed. and trans.) (Turin: Einaudi, 1969), p. 885; see also Claudio Magris' introductory essay to the same volume, 'L'esilio del borghese', in particular p. *xxiii* onwards.

not cruel, Proust organizes within the narrative context festive gatherings contemporary to him; and in order to descend into them as a spy—to possess and incorporate them—takes the stance of a protagonist of the festivals of yesteryear: namely, of eighteenth-century festive gatherings, which although already on the outer border of crisis, were still somewhat similar to a true festival. Thus, while disbelieving the possibility of a present-day festival, he deems it useful to identify with the participant in a true festival—an identification that is advantageous for him, at the point of coincidence between present historical time and stilled ahistorical actuality that is the point of his operating existence.

In harmony with the paradoxical nature of the artistic operation, and itself paradoxical, Proust's behaviour is very close to that of most modern ethnologists vis-à-vis the festivals of the *others*—except that the latter behaviour, having no access to the vantage point of 'art', constantly risks falling into inconsistency and superficial arbitrariness. Faced with the festivals of the *others*, these ethnologists remain incognito through masks and disguises which act outwardly (towards the *others* they approach while doing 'fieldwork') as simulacra of an identity with 'the primitives', and inwardly (towards the 'I' and the rest of their own civilized community) as an awareness of a shared humanity, a solidarity despite difference, an incognito quality of the 'I' that becomes the protagonist of a mask as soon as it accepts to become the protagonist of an objective knowing—and does not risk betraying that mask, since that mask, that 'objective knowing', rules and constrains those who take it on:

'Don't be afraid anyone might speak or behave in a manner unsuited to the costume he wears: it's the costume itself that makes that impossible!'[33]

'The important thing is not the play-acting': here it is not, and it cannot be, a matter of trust in the objective homology of the mask of the ethnologist camouflaged as a 'primitive' with the mask of the 'primitive' who takes on the semblance of the bison or the forest spirit; nor can it be a matter of real trust in the ethnologist's ability to accept himself and have others accept him as one who truly 'acts' the festival. The important thing is not the acting, but rather 'the moving while remaining unseen, the spying, the being recognized so as to hide'. For the ethnologist, the important thing is to move like an invisible being among the *others*, to spy on them, to become visible to their eyes as an 'other' who pretends to be 'alike' and whose fiction can be accepted. Thus the ethnologist doing 'fieldwork' needs visibility and invisibility in equal measure. He needs to be an invisible observer, an invisible spy of the *others'* otherness, and at the same time someone the *others* can see as other from them, but legitimately wearing the guise of someone 'alike': a stranger who may legitimately take on the semblance of an insider.

The model of this *facies* to be taken on in order to 'do fieldwork' is not, however, a mere consequence of the objective characteristics of the situation of the *others* with whom the ethnologist wishes to interact, especially on the occasion of their festivals. Rather, it is the result of the paradoxical interaction between two *othernesses*, peculiar respectively to the 'savages' and to the 'civilized'

---

33 Hoffmann, 'Il cuore di pietra', p. 886.

ethnologist. A stranger to the festivals of the *others*, the ethnologist can do no more than organize them within his own framework of scientific knowledge according to gnoseological models that in fact interact with the otherness of the *others*. He is a spy, but within a sphere that he himself composes and arranges, according to a given gnoseological model, as soon as he penetrates it. Thus he is a spy within a sphere that he himself has organized: a sphere that is such, and organized, only as soon as, and only because, he penetrates it as a spy. Within that sphere, the only autonomous material in the ethnologist's organizing / spying is the otherness of the *others*: the fact that the *others* are objectively liable to be spied upon. Otherness and spiability of the *others* are one and the same thing: it is in fact not possible to spy on anything but the *other*. It is not possible to penetrate the sphere of the 'alike' without being recognized—which also means: it is not possible to spy unseen on one's own 'I' and on what is identical to it.

But, in this regard, we need to return to the features described by Starobinski relative to eighteenth-century festive gatherings, in which it was important not only to 'spy' and to 'move unseen' but also to be 'recognized while remaining hidden'. The modern ethnologist faced with the festivals of the *others* finds himself in an analogous situation, even though we might want to note his relationship with his peers upstream from, or side by side with, his relationship with the 'savages'. If, at a more or less conscious level, ethnographic and ethnological research stems from the need for a gnoseological insight into one's own 'I' and its relationship with one's peers, investigations of the festivals of 'savages' satisfy that need insofar as they allow the 'I' to enter into a gnoseological relationship with *others* who work as counterfigures both for the 'I' and for the peers of the one who says 'I'. True, the 'savages' at their festivals are *other*, and in fact reach the maximum concentration of their otherness precisely in the festival; but precisely because the festival is the peak of their human peculiarity, while in the state of festival they also possess and exhibit the highest concentration of their universal humanness. They are, in short, 'men like all others', and exceptionally so, precisely when they are at their most *other*. At its maximum concentration, humanness paradoxically coincides with the peak of otherness. This allows the incognito descent among the *others* at their festivals, as well as into the depths of one's 'I'—making it possible to be a visible/invisible spy. But, as we have observed, each incognito descent into one's own 'I' is destined to be unmasked by the 'I' itself. This particular *katabasis* allows one to avoid a drastic unmasking and to maintain the position of the incognito spy, who is nonetheless recognized as he hides and yet remains incognito, since the 'savages' at their festivals are also counterfigures of those who are 'alike'—not *alike* in an absolute sense: but *alike* vis-à-vis the modern ethnologist who, lacking non-cruel collective experiences, has nobody truly *alike* but only *formerly alike*. The *others* ('savages') at their festival have allowed modern man to spy, through them, on those *formerly like* him.

Spied upon in the 'savages', the festival has thus worked to reinstate a direct relationship with the *formerly alike*; 'civilized' modern man has set about finding his own 'civilized' peers, turned into *others*, through the 'savages' at their festivals. In the collective experience of the non-cruel festival of the 'savages', the ethnologist has a newfound occasion to relate to the collective experience that he has lost with regard to his peers, *formerly* and no longer 'alike'. Conversely, and at the same time, he has found in the non-cruel festival of the 'savages' an occasion to somewhat distance himself from his own 'I', to spy upon it, insofar as identification of that 'I' with those *formerly like* it—via their 'savage' counterfigures—has allowed him to declare that 'I is an other' while referring to a concrete experience.

However, what we have been saying about the ethnologist being a stranger vis-à-vis the festival of the 'savage' *others* can also be used to stand our previous position upside down: thus the festival would not be a situation coming to encounter the ethnologist from the sphere of the *others*, allowing him to use the *others* as counterfigures of those *formerly alike* and of the 'I', but rather the situation into which the ethnologist plunges the *others* so as to use them for the purpose of rediscovering, through them, both solidarity with his peers and deliverance from solidarity with his own 'I'. Can these two interpretations be configured dialectically? Or at least: what might be the sense of configuring them dialectically (and of finding the limit to knowability of the festival in the tension between the two contrasting models, if not in their improbable synthesis)?

In the essay *La festa e la macchina mitologica*, we have tried to answer these questions, formulating them within the specific (but not entirely arbitrary) reference framework of issues relative to myth[34] and recording any answers that mechanically ensued from the simple fact of posing the problem within that framework. Given their particular origin, such answers had the advantage of arising as organically interrelated in such a way as to compose the gnoseological model of the 'mythological machine', in which it is possible to find the maximum common denominator between the manifold doctrines of the 'science of myth' or of 'mythology'.

It now remains to be seen whether not limiting the formulation of our questions about the festival to the reference framework of issues relative to myth, but posing them instead within the general (anthropological in the global sense) scope of the human sciences, might enable us to find (and find useful) the possibility of configuring the tension between the two contrasting models within the model of an 'anthropological machine'. We shall then also have to see whether the 'anthropological machine' is one aspect of the 'mythological machine', or whether both are aspects of one 'gnoseological machine'—or, finally, whether the affinity between the two 'machines' is merely a superficial one.

## 3. THE ANTHROPOLOGICAL MACHINE

The 'anthropological machine' (we shall hereafter dispense with the use of quotation marks for expressions such as mythological, anthropological, gnoseological *machine*, etc., taking as given their valency as designations

---

34 Furio Jesi, *Il mito* (Milan: ISEDI, 1973). [For a new edition, with a note by Giulio Schiavoni, see Jesi, *Mito* (Turin: Nino Aragno Editore, 2009).]

of models) is meant to be the complex mechanism producing images of man, anthropological models referring to the 'I' and to others, in all possible varieties of *otherness* (i.e. of extraneousness to the 'I'). Such models are rationally appraisable; not so, however, what is meant to be at the core of the machine, its immoveable mover: man, whether 'I' or another, and in fact other even when it is 'I'. All the numberless *others*, whose gnoseological models issue from the anthropological machine, and hence all the images of man that man can know, may be either epiphanies of *real* man (whether or not he is known: of real man as such, of the symbol—resting upon itself— of universal man) meant to be found inside the machine and to keep it working and producing by his presence; or the result of the production of the *empty* machine. The uncertainty as to whether the anthropological machine may be empty or full, may or may not possess an inner, immoveable prime mover, derives from the impenetrability of its walls. Such impenetrability is a premise, valid as a *conditio sine qua non*, of the gnoseological usability of the anthropological machine model: if the walls of the machine were in any degree transparent, one could establish to the same degree of exactness whether the machine were empty or full. But the margin of gnoseological usability of the anthropological machine model is precisely determined by the function of the model as configuring two contrasting hypotheses (neither of which we wish to lose) on the *emptiness* vs *fullness* of the machine: on the efficient existence vs efficient non-existence of the symbol—resting upon itself—of universal man. Further, the gnoseological impenetrability of the walls of the machine is posited because, otherwise, the very object on which both hypotheses hinge could not be configured within a dual outcome logic. The *efficient* existence of the symbol *resting upon itself* of universal man is a pure paradox within a dual outcome logic: a symbol *resting upon itself*, assuming it exists, is necessarily *inefficient* within such logic. Both hypotheses hinge on the efficient existence vs efficient non-existence of universal man: the inefficient existence of universal man as a pure symbol resting upon itself is beyond the limits of the problem. But, within a dual outcome logic, if universal man does really exist as a symbol resting upon itself, then he exists in an inefficient way, and therefore the knot is severed: the efficient existence of universal man, a symbol resting upon itself, is not there—thus the first hypothesis is discarded as false.

The stimulus to sacrifice neither contrasting hypothesis—hence the stimulus to use a model such as the anthropological machine—stems, as we have begun to see, from the relationship between the ethnologist (anthropologist) and the festival; it is mainly through the phenomenology of such stimulus that we can verify what the model is and what its possible use may be. To set out the two hypotheses once again: (1) the festival is a situation coming to encounter the ethnologist from the sphere of the *others*, allowing him to use the *others* as counterfigures of those *formerly alike* and of the 'I'; (2) the festival is the situation into which the ethnologist plunges the *others* for the purpose of rediscovering, through them, both solidarity with his peers and deliverance from solidarity with his own 'I'. The stimulus to sacrifice neither hypothesis (hence to have recourse to a non-dual logic that would not immediately exclude either, i.e. the anthropological machine model) stems from the need to negate neither that the sphere of the *others* gives rise to an encounter with the observer (such encounter being crystallized in the festival), nor that the observer effects an exploitation of the *others* (through plunging them into the festive state).

The phenomenology of this stimulus and of this need can be studied in two particularly important aspects of the festival, the *peaceful festival* and the *war festival*, as they appear to the eyes of those who legitimize sub-division of humankind into 'savages' or inferiors and 'civilized' or superiors. Clearly, this stimulus and this need are not in the least determined by the situation of those who deem such subdivision legitimate—and who seldom ask themselves our kind of question. Their attitude is in fact determined by the gross, racist and colonialist aspects of attitudes that have matured within European culture and have otherwise attained far higher levels of scientific seriousness and ethical dignity—of intellectual criticism, in short—such as to evince precisely that stimulus and that need. But, precisely because they are gross and exceedingly boorish, those racist and colonialist attitudes are, *mutatis mutandis*, most revealing of the mechanism which, when transposed to an entirely different level, induces the non-racist, non-colonialist ethnologist to search for a gnoseological model excluding neither the encounter (proceeding from the sphere of the *others* towards the observer, and useful to him) nor the exploitation of the *others* on the part of the observer: neither the force that pushes the sphere of the *others* to be usable, nor the force the observer exerts upon that sphere in order to use it.

## 4. Peaceful Festival and War Festival

In the early days of ethnography—from Jean de Léry, from André Thevet, to Père Lafitau (see Materials 2 and 3)[35]—the *peaceful festival* of the 'savages' was described as the moment in which the best qualities of such 'savages' shone forth in their fullness and greatest purity. The peaceful festival (hence all the manifold festivals not directly connected to war activities) is the moment in which the 'savage', at times in contrast with his more frequent behaviour, shows himself as meek, subject to joyful or mournful emotion, capable of singing in a strange but touching way, etc. Since however the 'savage' is an inferior and primitive creature, even his best qualities are vitiated by the coarseness of undisciplined instincts: his joy tends to turn into orgiastic feeling, his meekness translates into the quiescent state of basic animal satisfaction (whether induced by food or inebriating drink, sexual practices, etc.). This does not prevent the 'civilized' observer acknowledging, on certain occasions, that he is witnessing some noble sentiments (affection, melancholy, generosity, tender caring for the dead, etc.). The basic goodness of natural man (a concept that was certainly not invented by Rousseau) allows even men of undisciplined instincts to show some virtue. Père Lafitau goes as far as to stress the courtesy and respect for the niceties of manners shown by the 'American savages' at their festivals—'savages' who, in this regard,

---

35 See William Strachey, *The Historie of Travaile into Virginia Britannia* [1612] (L. B. Wright and V. Freund eds) (London: Ashgate, 1953); Robert Beverley, *The History and Present State of Virginia* [1705] (L. B. Wright ed.) (Chapel Hill: University of North Carolina Press, 1947); also Alan C. Taylor, *Le Président de Brosses et l'Australie* (Paris: Boivin, 1937).

he declares are often superior to his French contempo-
raries. (It's true, on the other hand, that for Père Lafitau
the 'American savages' are not exactly men who have
never left their natural state but rather the last survivors
of the Mediterranean 'Pelasgians', who reverted to their
savage state once they landed in America).

And the peaceful festival of the 'savages', in its
peculiar virtuous aspects, coincides with the models
of proper celebration (or even 'holy observance') of
festivals elaborated for their 'non-savage'—albeit often
'inferior'—compatriots not only by the Protestant
Rousseau but also by a Catholic moralist such as Canon
Capecelatro, in Naples, at the end of the eighteenth
century (see Appendices I and II to *La festa*). Such
celebrations of peaceful festivals among the 'civilized'
are naturally different from those of the 'savages', but
solely by the elimination of a presumed coarseness, by a
more carefully calculated balance, or by the paternalism
of their enforcement on the part of the authorities.

The peaceful festival of the 'savages' will in the end
translate, with Rousseau, into the emblem of the collective experience (of men still scarcely corrupted) in which
peace and joy, or even peace and sorrow, are real because
shared by all. Unlike most seventeenth- and eighteenth-
century ethnographers, Rousseau will, for that matter,
give special attention to festivals that are not only
peaceful but *joyful* (the peaceful and mournful *festival of
the dead*, a recurring *topos* in the observations of early
ethnographers, thus loses some of its prominence).[36] For

---

36 Furio Jesi, 'Della lettera X della parte IV de *La Nouvelle Héloïse* di
Jean-Jacques Rousseau', Appendix I to *La festa*; see also *Lettre à*

Rousseau, the festival of the 'savages' is already a suspension of work par excellence: on the one hand, it displays a refusal of corrupting work, motivated by greed and enforced as an obligation that destroys human dignity; on the other hand, it is the pause that gives rhythm to the phases of necessary, non-corrupting work developing human potential, and that allows (or in fact *is*) an access to the storehouse of latent energy implicit in the state of peaceful joy and cyclical deliverance from the conditioning of 'having to be'. The peaceful festival of the 'savages', who in Rousseau's imagination dance merrily around a maypole decked with flowers, is the moment in which man is without 'having to be'. The festivals of the French Revolution (Appendix IV),[37] although at least partly inspired by Rousseau's model, will belie that model insofar as they will become emblems of a collective 'having to be'. The Festivals of the Goddess Reason and

---

*d'Alembert*, and our considerations in the Epilogue to the same volume. 37 With respect to the text quoted in Appendix IV to *La festa*, note Thiers' derogatory tone towards the festivals of the Revolution, similar to that used by those who describe the festivals of 'savages' (*Robespierre 'avait la tête couverte de plumes'*) and are inclined to identify 'the people' as such with 'the savages'. From Rousseau's '*bon savage*' to the 'bad savage'—the 'bad faith savage': '*Mais quand le peuple est-il de bonne foi?*'— of which the people is composed.

The Musée Carnavalet in Paris holds prints and watercolours representing the festivals of Reason and of the Supreme Being. On Revolution festivals, see François Boissy d'Anglas, *Essai sur les fêtes nationales* (Paris: Imprimerie Polyglotte, An II, 1793); Antoine Français de Nantes, *Esprit des fêtes sans-culottides* (Paris: An II, 1793); Joseph Marie Lequinio, *Des fêtes nationales* (Paris: Imprimerie nationale, An III, 1794); and in general the works listed in the bibliography by Edmond Soreau, 'Les cultes révolutionnaires. Leurs origines' and 'La religion et la révolution française' in *Histoire générale des religions*, VOL. 4 (Maxime Gorce and Raoul Mortier eds) (Paris: Bloud et Gay, 1952).

of the Supreme Being will be moments in which the structure of the exemplary society, and hence of the exemplary 'having to be', will be *represented* by all in the presence of all.

Among the festivals of the 'savages', the 'civilized' observer has always seen war festivals as those where the 'having to be' comes closest to the surface (Materials 4). For 'civilized' man, warlike activity cannot but be a duty—and in fact one of the most salient examples of duty par excellence. It is a duty to fight for the sovereign, for the fatherland, for the ideal, for one's class, etc. Consequently, not even the 'savage' can find in the war festival a moment of deconditioning, of being without 'having to be'; rather, the war festival will be the moment in which one's duty [to fight] finds its ritual confirmation and representation. For analogous reasons, even a peaceful but mournful festival (a *festival of the dead*) is not a valid example of deconditioning: a mournful festival, even when it has nothing to do with a war against human foes (for example against the killers of the men being mourned), nonetheless remains the celebration of a defeat in the war of existence against death, and thus has as its backdrop—if not as its immediate subject of representation—a precise 'having to be', which can also be described as 'having to not die'.

In the war festival the 'savage' reveals the worst side of his instincts—his 'malice', his 'cruelty', his 'ferocious appetite for blood', etc. (and faced with war festivals, early ethnographers are generally left horrified); on the other hand, in the war festival the 'savage' belies the ideal of the festival as a deconditioning, a pause from work, as being without 'having to be' (and faced with this, Rousseau takes a stance of refusal, or just keeps silent).

The 'savage' is worthy of some respect as long as he is meek (though for early ethnographers his meekness is countered by excesses of undisciplined instinct); when he shows himself as ferocious, the 'savage' is abominable (though early ethnographers do not omit hints to his pride, courage, etc.). The 'savage' engaged in a peaceful festival comes to encounter the 'civilized' observer, offering himself to his knowledge as a human model that is imperfect but not devoid of virtue—a model such as can be used as an edifying and critical touchstone for corrupt 'civilized' man. The 'savage' at his war festival refuses to make himself known to 'civilized' man, just as the *mysterium iniquitatis* eludes knowledge; in the state of war festival, the 'savage' carries within himself, in the highest potency, all the vices corresponding to the war virtue of 'civilized' man when it is stripped of motivations such as justice, honour, etc.

To return to the two hypotheses that, while contrasting, may paradoxically be accepted together if we intend to make use of the anthropological machine model: (1) the festival is a situation that, from the sphere of the *others*, comes to encounter the ethnologist and allows him to use those *others* as counterfigures of those *formerly alike* and of the 'I'; (2) the festival is the situation into which the ethnologist plunges the *others* so as to be able to use them for the purpose of finding anew, through them, both solidarity with his peers and deliverance from solidarity with his own 'I'. In the phenomenology of the approach to the peaceful festival of the 'savages', hypothesis No. 1

seems to be actualized. The peaceful festival is known as a periodical suspension of representation and of 'having to be': it is the moment in which the image of man engaged in a virtuous collective experience surfaces towards the ethnologist from the sphere of the universally human. Symmetrically, hypothesis No. 2 is actualized in the phenomenology of the approach to the war festival. The war festival is a periodical repetition of the moment in which representation and 'having to be' reach their maximum intensity: it is the moment in which the ethnologist plunges the *others* into the sphere of their otherness (a sphere he has created), so as to recognize in them humanity in a state of guilt, of uncivilization, of 'instinctive' ferocity, etc.—hence also to rediscover within that sphere those (ethically negative) situations in which all men form a collectivity held together by solidarity in vice. That collectivity, when in a state of 'savage' war festival, also allows the ethnologist to split his 'I' in two: 'I' is an other, because it is absorbed into the entirety of the universally human, of the solid human mass caught at the height of its ferocity, and hence into a state of radical *otherness* with respect to the ethnologist's 'civilized' self. In the 'I' of the ethnologist is the 'I' of the 'savage': the ethnologist can observe him with detachment, separating himself from him, because the ethnologist is 'civilized'. The observer's gaze is 'civilized'; the observer's 'I' is 'savage'. The difference between 'I' and gaze is all the more relevant in that the 'I' shows itself as 'savage' in relation to what functions as a touchstone of civilization, i.e. representation and 'having to be'. In the sphere to which the ethnologist's gaze belongs, the more drastically

aggressive aspects of representation and 'having to be'—
first and foremost war, the adversary's elimination, etc.—
are also extremely 'civilized': war is 'righteous', 'heroic',
it is the 'dutiful' elimination of the aberrant, dangerous
individual. 'Savage' war (and by *war* we mean any
aggressive act organized by any group against any other)
vs 'civilized' war: in this contraposition we can pinpoint
the terms of the contrast between the ethnologist's 'I' and
his gaze. Using the *others*, plunging them into the state of
war festival, is done precisely to create a gnoseological
reference framework for this contrast.

## 5. Festive Action, Festive Time

The knowability of the festival also presents another
polarity that, at a first glance, might be deemed extraneous to the one we have described above between the
observer's 'I' and his gaze. This is the contraposition
between festive *action* and *time*, as starting points and
characterizing elements of two different gnoseological
models.

> In *Theory of the Leisure Class*, Thorstein Veblen notes:
>
> Presents and feasts had probably another origin
> than that of naive ostentation, but they required
> their utility for this purpose very early, and they
> have retained that character to the present [ . . . ].
> Costly entertainments, such as the potlatch or the
> ball, are peculiarly adapted to serve this end.[38]

---

38 Thorstein Veblen, *La teoria della classe agiata* (Franco Ferrarotti trans.)
(Turin: Einaudi, 1971) / *The Theory of the Leisure Class* (New York: B.
W. Huebsch, 1922).

Veblen's attention is not addressed to the *time* of the festival, to the festival as a periodical moment, or in any case to the relationship between festival and time, but rather to festive action. In Veblen's context, a festival is a certain behaviour belonging to the categories of 'naive ostentation' and 'conspicuous waste'. It is festive to behave with naive ostentation or conspicuous waste, independent of the collocation within time, or perhaps against time, of such behaviour. Veblen does not, for that matter, casually or superficially lose sight of the temporal dimension of the festival, but rather concerns himself by deliberate choice with considering festive action from the point of view of its 'profane' consequences (that there might have been a different perspective, whether sacred or in any way such as to accord special respect to an element overriding any social prestige consequences, is acknowledged by Veblen with the words: 'Presents and feasts had probably another origin than that of naive ostentation'). As noted by J. K. Galbraith,

> In fact, Veblen's anthropology and sociology are weapon and armour rather than science. He uses them to illuminate (and to make ridiculous) the behaviour of the most powerful class—the all-powerful class—of his time.'[39]

In his eyes, the festive behaviour of the 'all-powerful class of his time' was connected to the temporal dimension only insofar as it mirrored the conviction (on the

---

39 John Kenneth Galbraith, 'Thorstein Veblen e la teoria della classe agiata', *Comunità* 171 (January 1974): 44–64; here, p. 57 / 'Thorstein Veblen and the Theory of the Leisure Class', Introduction to Thorstein Veblen, *The Theory of the Leisure Class: An Economic Study in the Evolution of Institutions* (Boston: Houghton Mifflin, 1973).

part of the dominant class) that such dimension was enclosed within brief boundaries, like a splinter of eternity that *was* eternity and within which only a brief dynamic sequence corresponded to the march towards success. The festival of the 'leisure class' taking place within that supposed splinter of eternity is a festival involved in a modest temporal dynamics. An immoveable feast, stilled as the *saeculum* of the 'leisure class' must be, that festival is to be studied as a rigid set of acts performed once and for all in order to effectively promote reputation and 'good fame'.

Let us now juxtapose Veblen's page to one by Walter Benjamin:

> The awareness that they are about to make the continuum of history explode is characteristic of the revolutionary classes at the moment of their action. The Great Revolution introduced a new calendar. The initial day of a calendar serves as a historical time-lapse camera. And, basically, it is the same day that keeps recurring in the guise of holidays, which are days of remembrance. Thus the calendars do not measure time as clocks do; they are monuments of a historical consciousness of which not the slightest trace has been apparent in Europe in the past hundred years. [40]

---

40 Walter Benjamin, 'Tesi di filosofia della storia' in *Angelus Novus* (Renato Solmi ed. and trans.) (Turin: Einaudi, 1962), p. 80 / Walter Benjamin, 'Theses on the Philosophy of History' in *Illuminations* (Hannah Arendt ed. and Harry Zohn trans.) (New York: Harcourt, Brace and World, 1968).

The final words of this quote ('of a historical consciousness of which not the slightest trace has been
apparent in Europe in the past hundred years'), apart
from the specific reference to Europe, seem to support
Veblen's choice regarding the opportunity of studying the
festivals of the 'leisure class' as festive action rather than
festive time. The 'leisure class' owns by now only clocks,
not calendars, and uses as calendars the clocks by which
it measures the timescale of its own route to success.
Turning his attention more to the one who 'remains
[ . . . ] man enough to blast open the continuum of history'
than to the 'leisure class', Benjamin addresses the festival
first and foremost as festive *time*. To his eyes, festive
action is nothing but any action in which one has the
consciousness of 'blast[ing] open the continuum of history'.[41] If in the outlook of Veblen's study a festival necessarily is an instance of 'conspicuous waste', Benjamin
sees as festive even only the following episode in the July
Revolution:

> On the first evening of fighting it turned out that
> the clocks in towers were being fired on simul-
> taneously and independently from several places
> in Paris. An eye-witness, who may have owed
> his insight to the rhyme, wrote as follows: 'Qui
> le croirait! on dit, qu'irrités contre l'heure / De
> nouveaux Josués au pied de chaque tour, /
> Tiraient sur les cadrans pour arrêter le jour'.[42]

This contraposition between knowledge of the festival as action vs time is in fact parallel to the contrast

---

41 Benjamin, 'Tesi di filosofia della storia'.
42 Benjamin, 'Tesi di filosofia della storia'.

between the ethnologist's 'I' and his gaze examined above. For Veblen, the festival as festive action is a gnoseological model negating any collective quality of the festivals under consideration (the selfish initiative of individuals, effective in the environment of a narrow community that is subjected to them rather than taking part in them as a protagonist, or at most taking part as a protagonist insofar as it recognizes its own subjection and generously gives its consent). For Benjamin, the festival as festive time is a gnoseological model implying as a *sine qua non* condition both collectivity and self-affirmation in the festive experience under consideration. The festival configured by Veblen is the festival of 'savages', whether the Papuan tribes (performing it out of 'naive ostentation') or the Vanderbilts and Astors ('conspicuous waste'). The festival configured by Benjamin is the festival of the 'civilized', who use calendars—the new calendars they have introduced—rather than clocks. From Benjamin's point of view, the Vanderbilts or Astors are savages with clocks hanging from their necks, who nonetheless use those clocks to tell the time ('What time is it?' = 'What is the time?'), whereas the 'civilized' are those who tell the time from the calendar. If we so much as reverse this relationship we find ourselves looking again at the contraposition between the ethnologist's 'I' and his gaze. 'Savages' are those who celebrate the festival in order to really know what time it might be on the calendar face of sacred time—and for them, as for the 'I' of the ethnologist adhering to them, this means reconnecting to the hour that is to time what a point is to space. The 'civilized', whose gaze is the gaze of the ethnologist, are those who use the festival in order to look—thus, if optics is not an opinion, also in order to be looked at, to be the subject of the looks from which 'good fame' will ensue.

A meeting point of the two gnoseological models of the festival, and also of the two models (respectively parallel to them) of the ethnologist's 'I' vs his gaze can be found in what we might define as the symbolic anthropology of Elias Canetti. In the paragraph he devotes to the 'festive crowd' in *Masse und Macht*, Canetti stresses *density* and *loosening* in the festive experience:

> There is abundance in a limited space, and everyone near can partake of it. The produce of all kinds of cultivation is exhibited in great heaps. [ . . . ] There is more of everything than everyone together can consume and, in order to consume it, more and more people come streaming in. [ . . . ] Nothing and no-one threatens and there is nothing to flee from; for the time being life and pleasure are secure. Many prohibitions and distinctions are waived, and unaccustomed advances are not only permitted but smiled upon. For the individual the atmosphere is one of loosening and not discharge. There is no common identical goal which people have to try and attain together. The *feast* is the goal and they are there.[43]

As shown by this quote, here Canetti is studying the festive crowd solely in relation to a peaceful festival. He can watch festive action and festive time at once, by using, as a common denominator for both, the symbol of

43 Canetti, *Massa e potere*, pp. 63–4.

*density*, placed within a context of participation in the 'common enjoyment' seen as a 'loosening' rather than a 'discharge':

> They live for this moment and work steadily towards it [ . . . ] By common enjoyment at this one feast people prepare the way for many future feasts [ . . . ] The feasts *call* to one another; the density of things and of people promises increase of life itself.'[44]

This common denominator allows him to circumscribe the festive experience within the morphological terms of social biology: the (peaceful) festival is for the social body the precise phase of the process of existence in which a density, or concentration, of consumable goods works as a guarantee and as an accelerator of survival. A privileged nourishing substance (*concentrated* consumable goods) and a privileged moment of absorption (the moment of concentration enjoyed with the *loosening*) guarantee and accelerate survival of the social body. Privileged substance and privileged moment come together in the (peaceful) festival. However, as Wölfflin would say, beauty is in the eye of the beholder. Substance and moment can come together in the beauty of the festival because in the eye of the beholder, the observer (Canetti the ethnologist, sociologist and anthropologist) there *are*, or at least there *operate*, symbolic crystals resembling the splinters of the devil's mirror lodged in the eye and heart of little Kai in Andersen's *Snow Queen*.[45]

---

44 Canetti, *Massa e potere*, p. 64

45 *The Stories of Hans Christian Andersen* (Diana Crone Frank and Jeffrey Frank eds and trans) (Durham, NC: Duke University Press, 2005).

Density, *the heap*, is the first symbolic crystal at work: granted, it is a symbol that 'rests upon itself', but it does so within the social body as within the eye of the beholder, or at least the observer believes it to be working within the social body, since he sees it at work within his own individual body, a microcosm to the group's macrocosm, a micro-anthropos to the macro- anthropos Canetti tends towards in his evocation of the crowd. Observing the macroanthropos, Canetti deems pathological the working of symbolic crystals that do not promote survival or promote it at the cruel expense of single individuals, parts of the social body. The war festival is a pathological phenomenon; not so the peaceful festival. The war festival encloses time within a dying moment; the peaceful festival opens time to the voice of festivals that '*call* to one another'. This call is the instinctive norm ruling survival of the individual or social body; and survival is thus an opening of time to collective duration, whereas the survival of an individual over his victims is an enclosure of time within individual duration, and individual duration is nothing but the macabre caricature of survival: nothing but the stroll among graves of a solitary man gloating about being alive while others are dead. According to an ancient image, tombs have performed on behalf of the individual the *swallowing*[46] function that should be the prerogative of the social body: they have swallowed up the others, just like the collectivity swallows the heaped goods during a festival. Yes, the individual who has survived is privileged,

---

46 See Waldemar Deonna, 'Eros jouant avec un masque de Silène', *Revue Archéologique* 5(1) (1916): 74–97; Furio Jesi, 'Bes e Sileno', *Aegyptus* (July–December 1962): 257–75; here, pp. 268–9.

precisely because he has survived—but he's going hungry. The others have been eaten—not by him, but by the tombs; that banquet has given sustenance—not to him, but to the tombs. The festival of tombs, the festival of the sole survivor, is the nucleus of the cruel festival we have outlined.

In Canetti's words, festive action (in a peaceful festival) is strictly allied with festive time. As we have seen, festive action is festive time: 'The feasts *call* to one another'. The solidarity between action and time also implies solidarity between the observer's 'I' and his gaze; or, if you like, the solidarity between the observer's 'I' and his gaze *determines* the solidarity between festive time and festive action. But the solidarity between the observer's 'I' and his gaze stems from the fact that the observer—in Canetti's case—is such only insofar as he looks first and foremost at his own self, a self that is a biological organism functioning in view of its own survival within collective time: the time in which the macroanthropos functions in view of its own survival.

### 6. 'POPULAR' FESTIVALS

While these provisional results of our investigation have circumscribed the functioning of the anthropological machine within a distinctly ethnological scope in which 'savages' appear, we are still to consider the functioning of the machine within the sphere of folklore. There are no real 'savages' in folklore, but rather 'civilized' people so close to the margins of civilization that, within their sphere of behaviour, civilization itself appears especially and intermittently rarefied in such a way as to oppose—

precisely on account of its scarce density—a modest
and occasionally permeable barrier to 'non-civilization'.
Clearly, this has been the case only in the outlook implicit
and necessary to the development of folklore studies as a
scientific discipline over the last two hundred years.

The 'popular' festival studied by folklorists should be
reconnected, within the perspective of our research, to
the medieval 'feast of fools' (Appendix III).[47] We repeat:

---

47 Its character of 'folly', i.e. of periodical, sacrilegious and licentious
antinomianism, was interpreted in modern times as a late surviving element of the *festival* as a suspension of historical time and of the norms
obtaining within it: a periodic (and revivifying?) return to a primordial
situation; see Carl Gustav Jung, 'Contributo allo studio psicologico della
figura del Briccone' in Paul Radin, Carl Gustav Jung and Károly Kerényi,
*Il briccone divino* (Neni Dalmasso and Silvano Daniele trans) (Milan:
Bompiani, 1965), pp. 179–83 [see 'On the Psychology of the Trickster
Figure' (R. F. C. Hull trans.) in Paul Radin, *The Trickster: a Study in
American Indian Mythology* (New York: Schocken Books, 1972)]; and
Harvey Cox, *La festa dei folli. Saggio teologico sulla festività e la fantasia*
(L. Pigni Maccia trans.) (Milan: Bompiani,1971) [see *The Feast of Fools:
A Theological Essay on Festivity and Fantasy* (Cambridge: Harvard
University Press, 1970)].

   Documents in: J. B. Du Tilliot, *Mémoires pour servir à l'histoire de
la fête des foux, qui se faisoit autrefois dans plusieurs églises* (Lausanne-
Genève: Bousquet, 1741)—which is the primary source for the section
on Jacques-Antoine Dulaure in Jesi, *La festa*, Appendix III; and
Ferdinando Neri, *Le abbazie degli stolti in Piemonte nei secoli XV e XVI*
(Turin: Loescher, 1902). In Appendix III, we have quoted a passage from
Dulaure, rather than from Du Tilliot, because Dulaure's attitude is espe-
cially significant to the historical course of the *knowability* of the festival:
Dulaure's is the polemical position of a member of the Convention
towards a festival that in his view summed up the corruption of the
Christian religion. Contrasting with the very righteous revolutionary
festivals, the Christian 'Feast of Fools' worked to illustrate the immorality
of traditional religion and of the clerics who abetted it. In this context,
Dulaure joins the description of the Feast of Fools to the mention of other
forms of 'licentiousness' and 'indecency' in Christian religiosity: flagel-
lations, naked processions, etc.—see Jacques-Antoine Dulaure, *Mémoires*

*within the perspective of our research*, i.e. from the point of view of an investigation on the knowability of the festival, and hence on the mechanisms and functioning of gnoseological models as applied to the festival. That is, we are not saying that the 'feast of fools' is of and by itself, irrespective of the function it performs within the phenomenon of knowability of the festival, the basic starting point of the historical genesis of folk festivals. Rather, the 'feast of fools' is the mirror directly reflecting the mid-point between the two hypotheses we have referred to above with regard to the phenomenology of a scientific approach to the festival. In the eye of the folklorist, the protagonists of folk festivals—mostly agricultural populations within 'civilized' modern areas— find themselves at an intermediate stage between 'savage' and 'civilized'. Their festivals are for the most part peaceful—for although they live in a state of rarefied 'civilization', they are enclosed within the sphere of 'civilization' and subjected to its virtuous constraints. These peaceful festivals[48] do not however fully belong to the category outlined in hypothesis No. 1 discussed earlier. In these festivals, we do not see an image of man in the state of virtuous collective experience surfacing from the sphere of the universally human towards the researcher, as would happen in the peaceful festivals of the 'savages': the reason being that the folk festival is known as a periodical suspension of 'having to be' involving those—the 'people', the land-working paupers,

---

de Dulaure, *avec une introduction par M.L. de la Sicotière* (Paris: Poulet-Malassis 1862).

48 See Vittoria Lanternari's *La grande festa. Storia del Capodanno nelle civiltà primitive* (Milan: Il Saggiatore, 1959).

etc.—who do not have the full right to periodically suspend their 'having to be', since they are (albeit in imperfect terms) part of 'civilization' and not 'savages'.

Besides, insofar as the folk festival is a *modern* festival and posits itself as non-cruel, it is in fact devoid of any authentic festive quality. A *modern* festival is not a collective festival, for there is no collective joyful festival in the socio-political scenarios of a culture that isolates the protagonists of folklore somewhere midway between 'the savages' and 'the civilized' (note that the cruel festival is not collective: not because—in a true collectivity— 'man is good', but because, tautologically, the festive sense is configured as a sort of joyful-collective expansion towards the duration of collectivity). Those who are not perfectly civilized are not civilized—they are essentially savages. Hence the singular paternalism of research on folklore, whether it sees the protagonists of folklore as inferior people or as 'companions' with strange and precious cultural prerogatives. In the latter case, it will perhaps be a paternalism contaminated by enthusiasm, admiration or sympathetic pathos towards the behavioural modalities of the oppressed. The gnoseological quality of these approaches is constantly vitiated by the quotidian, i.e. the non-festive par excellence, the matrix of an *a priori* contradiction, what is summed up in the perception of history as a *continuum*.

## 7. CONCLUSIONS

The quotidian, that which continually surrounds man, is not a scenario remaining fixed, or shifting only insofar as it decays and is renewed by a biological, physical, chemical law; rather, it is the paradoxical substance of an epiphanic rhythm: a rhythmical 'substance-force' (as R. Pettazzoni would define it[49]) which, when apprehended within the scope of science, is translated into the substance of a gnoseological rhythm. The difference between the 'ancient' or 'primitive' man who lives a festival and the modern scholar concerned with knowing the festival stems from the difference between epiphany and gnosis. The gnoseological rhythm, perceptible by the scholar, is the working rhythm of the anthropological machine. Since we in fact find ourselves in the position of the scholar and not in that of those who live the festival, we cannot formulate any serious hypothesis on what *might* be hiding behind the translucent walls of the anthropological machine. And the machine is working—working at its own peculiar rhythm, as defined by the revealing and concealing of the quotidian in terms of gnoseological (not epiphanic) experience. At the moment of its being revealed, the quotidian is the *other*; at the moment of his appearing in the festive state, man is the *other*. The quotidian in its concealed phase and man in his non-festive state are the known and the 'alike'. This is also true of the 'I' of the observer—the ethnologist. But the modern ethnologist does not have the faculty of revealing himself to himself, of appearing to himself in his festive state: he is therefore barred from access to his own 'I' insofar as such access presupposes a preliminary distance, a difference, between the observer and his own 'I' (or, in other words, between the 'I' and the self—where 'I' obviously stands

---

49 Raffaele Pettazzoni, *La confessione dei peccati*, VOL. 1 (Bologna: Zanichelli, 1929), p. 53.

for the observer, not the observed, the self). In order to know oneself, it is first and foremost necessary to split oneself and face one's 'I' (self) as if facing the *other*. One will then be facing something difficult to know (an other, precisely); but the festive experience will allow the actualizing of the paradox of knowing the other at the moment in which he is most other. All this is barred to the modern ethnologist. Lacking epiphanic experience, deprived of any images that are true revelations, the ethnologist can only work with *machines*, with functioning gnoseological models—the mythological machine, the anthropological machine—that purport to contain epiphanic images at their centre, as an inaccessible nucleus and immovable prime mover.

Is it legitimate, within scientific research, to credit what machines say or tacitly give one to understand regarding their purported invisible and immoveable prime mover? Nothing allows for an affirmative answer, although one must doubtlessly overcome a certain repugnance if accepting to replace—as subjects of study— *myth* with *mythological machine*, *man* with *anthropological machine*. One suspects however that this conclusion is in fact the hidden and camouflaged aim of the machines themselves, and hence the target of the social forces dominating the cultural situations within which machines are real and functioning. Machines seem to purport to contain inaccessible realities; but we cannot exclude that just this might be their cunning (i.e. the conservative force of the social dominants allowing the existence of the machines): alluding to an immovable prime mover precisely in order to be disbelieved, thus inducing belief solely in them, in machines, voids, barriers built from productive mechanisms that isolate one from what does not produce until the latter is rendered apparently non-existent.

But in order to discover whether this cunning of machines is truly such, and whether, beyond them, what does not produce actually *is*, it is necessary to destroy not machines themselves, which would reform like the heads of the Hydra, but rather the situation that makes machines real and productive. The possibility of this destruction is exclusively political; the risk it involves, from a gnoseological point of view, is that machines might really be empty and that thus their vacuity, once revealed, might impose itself as a paradoxical negative machine producing nothingness from nothingness. This is not however a real risk, since for now, before the destruction, it is impossible for us to formulate any plausible hypothesis about the afterwards (even the expression 'a negative machine producing nothingness from nothingness' is tied to the present, it is the *predictable present*, and thus the most improbable future). Besides, destroying the situation that makes machines—the 'anthropological machine', the 'mythological machine'— real and productive means pushing beyond the boundaries of bourgeois culture, not just trying to slightly deform its border barriers. The impossibility of the festival as a true collective moment derives, at present, from the peculiar features of bourgeois society; the non-knowability of the festival derives, at present, from the features of the culture matured and expressed by that society (precisely, and not by chance, the same society and culture that appear to have taken great care to preserve the tradition of festivities). Our discourse has so far focused specifically on outlining this phenomenon.

Having examined its unfolding, our attitude is not one of nostalgia for the collective festivals that we imagine took place in the past or in cultures different from ours. We do not know the possible positive or negative qualities of those festivals: the fact of having presumably been collective experiences does not necessarily attribute a positive character to them (there were and are collective actions and experiences noxious both to those who enacted them and those who suffered them). Neither can our stance accept as certain the hypothesis that in a society different from bourgeois society, in a society born of a socialist revolution, the degree of collectivity reached by experiences of existence and culture may be directly proportional to a recovered festive quality and to an increased knowability of the festival. The walls of the anthropological machine remain impervious and prevent any sensible forecast. At the same time, our present non-knowledge of the festival stops us assessing the latter as good or bad from a political and social point of view. As for the increased knowability of the festival that might perhaps derive from the increased possibility of festive experience, it is pointless at present to wonder whether that would be good or bad *in itself.* The gnoseological problem cannot be isolated, made autonomous, separated from the political and social problem: a higher degree of knowability of the festival can be good or bad only in a scenario where (not *insofar as*) one can concretely experience as good or bad an increased possibility of festive experience in the context of a different society.

# 'Cesare Pavese and Myth: "Dix ans plus tard" (Notes for a Lecture)'

EDITOR'S NOTE

On 21 February 1972, Jesi wrote to Franco Mollia:[1]

> I myself (being at present unable, for various reasons, to return to this subject) would be inclined to speak of Pavese 'the moralist', and hence of a basic immobility in Pavese's experience of the symbols (and troubles) that were salient for him, in singular continuity, from 'The South Seas' onwards. In fact I'd say it might be worth speaking of a very real hypnosis that those symbols exerted on Pavese, forcing him, by way of their immobility, into a radicalization of his ethical attitude.

These words touch on the theme of the morals of sacrifice and of *religio mortis*, and are thus connected to Jesi's early essays on Pavese, written between 1964 and 1966 and collected in *Letteratura e mito*,[2] on myth as the 'tie that bound ἔθος to μῦθος', either as guilt or as the 'obscure law enforcing morals, duty, death.' And on the other hand, they find a precise correspondence in the epilogue to *Il mito*[3] in which Jesi writes that to voice any pronouncement on the existence or non-existence of myth means 'to be subjected with scant defences to the very real hypnosis the mythological machine exerts around itself'. The letter is useful, for both these reasons, to the purpose of introducing and positioning the essay 'Cesare Pavese and

---

1 Franco Mollia (1923–2015), scholar, lecturer and author of several monographs on contemporary Italian writers, including a comprehensive essay on Pavese's *oeuvre* published in 1963. [Trans.]

2 Jesi, *Letteratura e mito*. [Trans.]

3 Jesi, *Il mito*. [Trans.]

Myth: "Dix ans plus tard"' in this volume; and it also sounds like an unspoken but fully honoured promise: the following text was first published in 1976, in the journal *Il lettore di provincia* (25–26), of which Franco Mollia was one of the editors.[4]

---

4 On the writing of this essay, and in general on Jesi as an interpreter of Cesare Pavese, see also Gianni Venturi, 'Cesare Pavese, Furio Jesi e il mito: una interpretazione' in *Cesare Pavese: atti del convegno internazionale di studi* (Torino: Santo Stefano Belbo, 24–27 October 2001 / Florence: Leo S. Olschki, 2005), pp. 77–110.

# Cesare Pavese and Myth: 'Dix ans plus tard' (Notes for a Lecture)[1]

*Dix ans plus tard*: a formula after the manner of Dumas,[2] justified by the fact that almost exactly ten years have passed since the critical debate on the connections between Cesare Pavese and myth was—I wouldn't say opened, but certainly reopened and invested with a different and much greater significance. December 1964: publication of a monographic issue on Pavese of the journal *Sigma*.

## 'PROGRESS' OF CRITICISM

Let us think of a historian of medicine, a discipline in whose historical course the notion of 'progress' seems to always have had a rather concrete, precise meaning. For a historian of medicine, it will no doubt be very important to reflect, first and foremost, both on the history of scientific thought in general and on the technical field, whose changes have determined the foregrounding of one or the other prophylactic, diagnostic or therapeutic

---

1 A lecture delivered by Jesi at the Universities of Lausanne and Sankt Gallen on 1–2 December 1975.

2 Jesi introduces a note of levity by alluding to the last of Alexandre Dumas' d'Artagnan Romances, *Dix ans plus tard* [*Ten Years Later*], published in 1847. [Trans.]

problem. Clearly, the same historian of medicine will need to consider not only the history of her own instruments but also the history of diseases, of their changes, and of their interactions with all the other components of the social, cultural and economical history of human groups. The same historian of medicine, if more traditional, less Foucauldian, will at times realize that her own notion of progress is not as obvious as it might seem; and that even where it appears credible, this progress cannot be investigated solely in light of the history of scientific instruments as such. Yet in the field of medicine, the word 'progress' retains a certain concreteness and precision: to heal the greatest possible number of diseases, to the greatest extent and in the greatest depth possible. Or—if we wish to circumvent the hurdle of defining a disease—to prevent death. That's something quite concrete and precise.

But if even for a historian of medicine it is important not to blandly accept a generic notion of progress and not to be hypnotized by the historical vicissitudes, as such, of the instruments used by the physician, think how important the same careful attitude must be for a historian of literary criticism—a historian, that is, of an intellectual activity which, in its wider sense, is tasked not so much with preventing death but with recognizing and continually knowing the life of a living thing. And this living thing, the writer's work, offers the critic not one, but endless different points of arrival.

The critic must not only avoid being hypnotized by the apparent vicissitudes of her instruments as such and by the illusion of progress that can stem therefrom, but also recognize that those vicissitudes, as such, are a pure abstraction devoid of historical existence; and must strive to seek out the reasons for the genesis and changes of critical instruments within the processes of interaction between the work of each writer and the history of those who recognize and know it as a living thing; their collective history, and their individual stories as well. For these reasons, to speak of Pavese and myth 'ten years later' will first and foremost mean, for me, to set out some reflections on the possible reasons (intrinsic both to Pavese's work and to our history, as well as to my own story) for which criticism can but continually return to Pavese's figure, no less alive and thus no less enigmatic than on the first day—so that (assuming we do not want to stop at building a monument on his tomb) its enigmatic character seems to be a precious value, and this criticism presents itself as a sort of collective work in progress. A diverse work in progress, in which even funerary monuments have their place—the place attributed to them, within this diverse complexity, by history, which is in fact the route and norm by which we delve, as critics, into criticism.

When I was at secondary school, Pavese was not yet a classic. Our anthology only included one of his poems: 'The South Seas'. In 1951–53, Pavese was the poet I heard my teacher, and other people in Turin, speak of as a friend who had recently died. He was not at all a statue, equal to all the others, in the gallery of the great. For precisely that reason I had the chance to read him in a curious, critical, and even judgemental way: almost—as I can say now, while certainly being unaware of it back then—to verify whether he deserved to be included in an anthology of the great, whether he really was a poet, that man who, relative to me, could not enjoy the privilege of distance, which is a feature characterizing crowned poets. And I clearly recall how that poem, 'The South Seas'—the only thing I was offered by way of an introduction to Pavese's work—left a contradictory, basically negative impression on me. On the one hand it seemed to me a poem that can be read with pleasure; on the other hand, it gave me the impression of a poem written by a man who wants to be a great poet, who wants to *act* the great poet—and might not be one.

What bothered me—I clearly recall that as well—as something forced and disharmonic was the contrast between the solemn musicality of the verses, somewhere between epic and lyrical, and their content—which, it seemed to me, remained on this side of that form, in our world, not in the world of great poets. Back then, my poetic ideal was Carducci[3]:

> *Sui campi di Marengo batte la luna; fosco*
> *Tra la Bormida e il Tanaro s'agita e mugge*
>     *un bosco;*
> *Un bosco d'alabarde, d'uomini e di cavalli,*
> *Che fuggon d'Alessandria da i mal tentati valli.*[4]

Or:

---

3 Giosuè Carducci (1835–1907), the 'national poet' of nineteenth-century Italy, whose poetics was firmly rooted in the classical tradition. The quatrains quoted by Jesi are from his collection *Rime nuove*, first published in 1887. [English translation: *The Rime Nuove of Giosuè Carducci* (Laura Fullerton Gilbert trans.) (Boston: Richard G. Badger, 1916)]. [Trans.]
4 From 'Sui campi di Marengo', narrating Frederick Barbarossa's failed siege of the Piedmontese town of Alessandria in 1174–75. Roughly translated as: 'The fields of Marengo lie white under the moon; / between the

*Su 'l castello di Verona*
*Batte il sole a mezzogiorno,*
*Da la Chiusa al pian rintrona*
*Solitario un suon di corno.*[5]

And I could find something of all this in Pavese's
poem, in its rhythm, its emphasis. But, by contrast, I
could also find things that were quotidian, not remote or
legendary enough: the emigrant cousin coming home, the
petrol pump, the collector's stamps. I would say—and of
course I would say it in today's words, words that can
only vaguely circumscribe the impressions I had back
then and that will doubtlessly cast those impressions in
an excessively solemn light—I would say that in Pavese's
poem I found something unfinished, something vitiating
the sort of moral aura I judged inseparable from true
poetry: the detachment from the quotidian, the moving
among absolute values ringing loud and clear that I could
find in Carducci but also, to mention another one of my
favourite readings at that time, in Vincenzo Monti's translation of the *Iliad*.

Was that completely wrong? I mean: Was that boy, back
in the early 1950s, really unable to understand Pavese's
classical greatness? Did that boy, back then, really lack
sufficient familiarity with modern literature, and was he

---

Bòrmida and the Tànaro [rivers] a forest seethes with gloom; / a forest
of men, of horses and halberds / fleeing Alessandria of the unshaken ramparts.' [Trans.]
5 From 'La leggenda di Teodorico', inspired by the legend in which the
Ostrogoth king Theoderic dies from being pitched by his horse into the
crater of a volcano. Roughly translated as: 'Over the castle of Verona /
The midday sun is glaring / from the Lock over the plain / a lone hunting
horn is blaring.' [Trans.]

too accustomed to outmoded patterns which stopped him accepting the lyricism of his contemporary poet?

That was certainly true, in part—but later I realized that my first critical impression had also held some truth. Later: that is, since I began to consider, in my capacity as a mythologist, Pavese's *oeuvre*, his relationship with myth, and what was known as 'the Pavese myth', the result of the mythological transfiguration of his figure.

What was that part of truth present in the judgement I passed as a child and later retrieved? Mainly this: the contrast between Pavese's conviction of finding in the repertoire of mythological images a poetic lexicon immanent in nature, and his deliberate choice of using that lexicon one way or another. To put it plainly: Pavese believed in the value of myths as a system of relationships existing in nature. In nature we can see manifold systems of relationships—for instance, between colours that can be transferred onto canvas when painting. In this respect, there is a significant passage in Hermann Hesse's novella *Klingsor's Last Summer*:

> And colours too may be altered—yes, they may be muted or enhanced, transposed in hundreds of ways. But when wishing to give a poetic interpretation of a part of nature through colours, one must retain within a hair's breadth the exact relationship, the difference in value between the two colours, as it is in nature. There is no escaping this point, one must remain veristic, no matter that one might use orange rather than grey or garanza lacquer rather than black. [6]

---

6 Hermann Hesse, *Klingsor's Last Summer* (Richard Winston and Clara Winston trans) (New York: Farrar, Straus & Giroux, 1970). [Trans.]

Clearly, I do not wish to derive from these words a law of landscape painting that cannot or must not be infringed, as Hesse seemed to be stating. I simply wish to point out that Pavese's attitude regarding mythological images was precisely that of Hesse's painter regarding the colours in nature. 'Colours may be altered', but 'one must retain within a hair's breadth the exact relationship, the difference in value between the two colours, as it is in nature.' In the same way, Pavese worked as if there existed in nature an objective system of relationships between mythological images that must be respected if one wishes—as Hesse would say—to 'give a poetic interpretation of a part of nature'. Mythological images may be altered, transposed in hundreds of ways; one may, so to speak, use orange instead of grey and garanza lacquer instead of black; but not alter the relationship, the difference in value, between mythological images. Otherwise one betrays a language that, like the language of colours, is immanent and objective in nature.

Regarding mythological language as immanent and objective in nature—some words from a discussion I once heard between Pasolini and Moravia: Pasolini said that one of the essential tasks of poetry, conferring purity onto poetry if attended to, consists of calling things by their name, calling the sea 'sea'. To which Moravia, in his usual sharp and seemingly somewhat bothered tone, replied that in fact the sea doesn't call itself 'sea', and that it is therefore not at all certain that its real name is 'sea'. This is it: for Pavese, the mythological image of the sea was the real name of the sea, the name objectively inherent to its essence in nature. So the poet wishing to speak of the sea relative to other elements and processes of nature was of course free to alter that image in any way he chose, but not to alter the relationship between that image and the images of the other elements, the difference in value between those mythological images as it is in nature. If he altered the image of the sea, so should he also alter all the others, in such a way as to maintain the same mutual relationship between them. Should we wish to multiply comparisons, we could obviously turn to the example of music and musical transposition—and this too would be a legitimate comparison, as long as we referred to those theories of music in which harmony is something objective and immanent in nature. Or we could turn to examples taken from mathematics, from the theory of numbers, provided again we referred to a system of mathematical thought according to which numbers possess their own existence, immanent and objective in nature.

It is not a question of establishing whether Pavese was right or wrong. That is a false problem: a poet is always right in the formulation of a theory of poetry, insofar as that theory serves him well. However, I have begun to outline Pavese's attitude towards mythological images in order to clarify a *contrast* that in my view is present in his work. The contrast is as follows: at the same time as he believed in the existence in nature of a system of relationships—that was a lexical system, a vocabulary—between mythological images, Pavese also believed in the impossibility for modern man to access a collective experience of myth. What does that mean? It means that for Pavese modern men are no longer able to experience all together, intimately, with the entirety of their being, the truth (objective and immanent in nature) of nature's vocabulary. This vocabulary, made of mythological images, can be accessed by modern man, whether or not he is a poet, at best individually, but not as a member of a community sharing in that abundance.

It follows that being in relation with those mythological images, feeling them as real, means being an individual who becomes increasingly separate from community; giving in to the temptation to access the language of nature means being the solitary beneficiary of an abundance that, if it is to have any humanistic value, should in fact be enjoyed by everyone through an act of collective sharing in which all can recognize themselves as part of a community.

There lies the contrast. On the one hand the poet, in order to be a poet, must, even before speaking *of* nature, speak *with* nature, in the language of nature, which is the language of myth. Only if he first knows the system of relationships objectively existing between mythological images can he then change those images while maintaining their relationships unaltered. But on the other hand the poet, in speaking *with* nature, becomes isolated from the human community, and is in fact subjected to an experience that takes full possession of him and overwhelms him in its totality, while demanding he make himself available to pleasures that run directly counter to collective humanistic values.

There's no way out. Or rather, the only way out is in accepting the myth most closely shorn of images: the myth of sacrifice. In the immense repertoire of mythological images, the myth of sacrifice is the one that can best be configured as a pure architecture of relationships, devoid of images; like a building with walls that do not exist, but that—if they did exist—would be set in a precise mutual relationship. It is the only myth in which the individual can be alone in his relationship with the language of myths, and nonetheless connected to his community because he *must* be alone, according to a law that is the law of his community. The myth of sacrifice is the only myth that allows one to face myth alone while being in accord with one's community—in times when a shared access to myth is impossible. But the myth of sacrifice is a death myth, and sacrifice is a mythical death. This is why I have repeatedly spoken of a religion of death in Pavese's work, and even in Pavese's person.

About ten years have passed since I first spoke of this *religio mortis* in Pavese, making use of my habitual study of mythological materials. The first time this expression, *religio mortis*, surfaced in my work with regard to Pavese was when I wrote the essay 'Cesare Pavese, il mito e la scienza del mito' for the 1964 issue of *Sigma*. Back then, one of the most characteristic reactions from reviewers was connecting my interpretation to the one given by Moravia in 1954, in his article 'Pavese decadente'.[7] One reviewer wrote: 'Jesi dismantles the mystifications used by Pavese to conceal his decadent nature leaning towards death.' But this was not the sense of my essay, and there was in fact much distance between my words and Moravia's. I have never used the expression 'decadent',

---

7 Originally published in *il Corriere della Sera* (22 December 1954), and later included in Alberto Moravia, *L'uomo come fine e altri saggi* (Milan: Bompiani, 1964), pp. 187–91. [Trans.]

which has always struck me as a dangerous common-place, about Pavese or anyone else. But my early essay might have given rise to that sort of misconstruction. It was in fact an experimental sounding in one particular direction—the relationship that Pavese, in a more or less indirect and unaware manner, had with some aspects of Mitteleuropean and especially German culture as he delved passionately and, one should add, responsibly into myth and the science of myth. Thus, my essay was in fact one-sided, leaving in shadow some aspects of that problem—which, for that matter, were examined in the same issue of the journal by Eugenio Corsini in his essay 'Orfeo senza Euridice: i *Dialoghi con Leucò* e il classicismo di Pavese'.[8]

This one-sidedness was, in my view, best understood by Gianni Venturi, who was in fact a specialist in the history of Pavese criticism, as well as a Pavese scholar. In a note published in the *Rassegna della letteratura italiana* in 1966, Venturi stressed the value of the distinction made by Corsini between the *two* classicisms in Pavese:

> A traditional type of classicism in which the harking back to the great writers of classical antiquity is inscribed in the span of Pavese's research on poetics and configured as a requirement pertaining to style and composition as well as to adhesion to an age-old tradition; and on the other hand, a restless, turbid classicism that can be viewed as heir to the various classicistic experiences of decadentism.

---

8 Eugenio Corsini, 'Orfeo senza Euridice: i *Dialoghi con Leucò* e il classicismo di Pavese', *Sigma* (1 December 1964): 121–46. [Trans.]

And, Venturi added, Pavese himself had situated the possibility of this twofold classicism 'in its three roots: classical culture proper (Virgil), classical culture as a component of the decadent climate and culture (D'Annunzio), and classical culture as ethnography and science of myth according to the theories of Kerényi and other mythologists.' 'Pavese's statement,' Venturi continued, 'is therefore itself indicative of a complexity, an interweaving of cultural suggestions that cannot be reduced to only one of its components.' Whereas my essay, without wishing to reduce either that 'complexity' or that 'interweaving of cultural suggestions' to 'only one of its components', undoubtedly delved deeper mainly into *one* of them. Hence also Venturi's reservations on some of my conclusions: 'Jesi notes how Pavese, not accepting, unlike Mann, to conceal his *religio mortis* by the mystification of "working for man", remained orthodox towards the religion of death in its most nihilistic aspects'. And he objected:

> Pavese's *oeuvre*, implicitly acknowledged for one surviving drive—the refusal to accept the ultimate mystification—cannot be accepted on these terms without turning him into a decadent, thus misrepresenting his historical importance and his teachings.

This note by Venturi (five pages long, but of far greater importance than its size would suggest as a precise refocusing of Pavese criticism, at a particularly delicate moment), was published in 1966, almost at the same time as my second essay on Pavese, 'Cesare Pavese dal mito della festa al mito del sacrificio'.[9] When I had occasion to read that note, I was glad that my second essay would clear the ground of the misconstructions caused by the first. Rereading my first essay and Venturi's polemical riposte today, I get the impression that the misconstruction consisted mainly of that concept, if not even of that one word, 'decadentism': a word I had not used, but that a specialist in the history of literature had every right to read as implicit in my essay. Writing that Pavese, in refusing Thomas Mann's mystification of 'working for man', had remained 'orthodox towards the religion of death in its more nihilistic aspects', I had used a language that in an essay of criticism and literary history might have been taken to clearly mean: Pavese was a decadent artist who with singular rigour remained faithful to the deep-seated nihilism of European Decadentism. That was not my intention—firstly because, as I have said, the very concept of decadentism did not and does not belong to my outlook on the history of culture. The 'more nihilistic aspects' of the religion of death towards which, I noted, Pavese was rigorously orthodox appear to me as the line circumscribing a myth of sacrifice and duty that is by its moral quality situated outside the character of what has been called 'decadentism' and its ideological and political implications—in other words, extraneous to the figure of the 'decadent' artist as defined in the iconography of the criticism that makes use of this concept. A concept which, I repeat, seems dangerous to me, precisely because it can entail generalizations and misconstructions similar to

9 See *Letteratura e mito* (1968). [Trans.]

those Venturi and I incurred, at least in the early stages of comparing our positions. As I said, I read Venturi's note at the time my second essay on Pavese was being published, and was glad that the essay could work as a sort of unwittingly clarifying reply—'clarifying', I mean, for myself, more than for him. Reading Venturi's review of my second essay, as well as the references he made to it in his later writings on Pavese, I could see we had understood each other perfectly. In his review, Venturi quoted a passage from my introductory notes to the three novels collected under the title *La bella estate*:[10]

> The dynamics internal to each of the three novels leads the young men from innocence to sin and later to sacrifice—which is not an atonement, but rather a necessity according to a moral law that promises no future salvation but offers a harsh, fatal virtue to those who submit to it.

And he saw in my observations one possible solution to what he deemed

> one of the most urgent problems in Pavese criticism, i.e. defining the suture point between myth and history, between moral teaching and exasperation of one's unhappiness. By interpreting Pavese's mythical solution as a moral one, Jesi fills the hiatus between the images of Pavese (the *engagé* vs the 'mythical'), between moral will and drawing back into oneself.[11]

---

10 Cesare Pavese, *La bella estate* (Turin: Einaudi, 1949) / *The Beautiful Summer* (W. J. Strachan trans.) (London: Peter Owen, 1955)].
11 *La Rassegna della letteratura italiana* 71(1-2) (January–August 1967): 307–08 [Trans.]

This was the key point: the fact that Pavese's orthodoxy towards the religion of death in its more nihilistic aspects signified, even in the (admittedly easy to misconstrue) words of my first essay, the experience of a sacrifice that is not an atonement, of a virtue that is 'harsh and fatal'. These were the 'more nihilistic aspects' of Pavese's *religio mortis*. And even today, 'ten years later', it still seems to me that a man will reach the bottom not of nihilism as such but of the nihilism *of a religion of death*, when, rather than refusing the existence of any virtue, he accepts— for himself—a harsh, and above all *fatal*, virtue. 'Nihilism of a religion of death' does not mean refusal of one's responsibilities as an artist and as a man; rather, it certainly means accepting those responsibilities in terms that are dangerous for oneself: and Pavese has shown just how severe and immediate the danger was. He has shown the great pressure brought to bear against him by that mythological image of human sacrifice—and I think we should stress even today that we do not know to what extent that image prevailed and to what extent it was chosen. In the note he left before dying, Pavese wrote: 'Don't gossip too much'. I think spending time more or less in vain on the effort of establishing whether his suicide happened through him being overwhelmed or through choice would be to 'gossip too much'.

## THE MOON AND THE BONFIRES AS A RECKONING WITH MYTHOLOGY

This was the last novel by Pavese, published in the year of his death. One is tempted to read it as a conclusive text, deliberately or involuntarily revealing of the human and artistic vicissitude of the author. In fact, *The Moon and the Bonfires* is a key text only because it is the point of confluence of most of the themes and images that recur in Pavese, almost a *summa* of his narrative.[12] Those themes and images have, however, often attained greater life and harshness in his earlier works, where they did not all appear together. Even the mode of narration has turned a corner: the elliptical, reticent narration, with its sharp openings into cry or elegy, with its shrugs cutting into dialogue, has made way for a wide-ranging, outspoken tone, as of communication offered with the same breadth throughout the novel, so that the tangle of themes and faces may acquire some organic order. Each theme and each image partially loses the dramatic charge that had characterized it in isolation so as to allow for mutual presence. At least, this is the intention. In fact, many of the flashes in the novel retain all their harshness (which clearly would have proved in no way tractable at any rate); but doubtlessly a new calmness has emerged, and the aggression is often contained or even extinguished.

Looking at Pavese's stylistic trajectory as a whole, my impression is however that the actual framework of the *novel* in a strict, traditional sense (not of the *story*, as in, for instance, *The Devil in the Hills*[13]) was not for Pavese at that time the most important objective, but rather a necessity determined by the task of channelling

---

12 Cesare Pavese, *La Luna e i Falò* (Turin: Einaudi, 1950) / *The Moon and the Bonfires* (Tim Parks trans.) (New York: Penguin, 2021).

13 Cesare Pavese, *Il diavolo sulle colline* (Turin: Einaudi, 1948) / *The Devil in the Hills* (R.W. Flint trans.) in *Selected Works of Cesare Pavese* (New York: NYRB, 2001).

much autobiographical matter (relating to both daily life and spiritual life) into calmed forms. Calmness was indispensable, for within that matter two components would fatally surface that in themselves are already a cry: the 'rootless' solitude of one who cannot recognize in the world anything to truly call his own (or anything that can truly claim him as its own), and the choice of death—where death is not to be intended as a 'solution', a remedy for solitude, but rather as the expression (in the form of an *obligation*) of the same force that has imposed that solitude.

Anguilla,[14] the character saying 'I' in the novel, is the foundling from the children's home, the fatherless, motherless waif plunged at a very young age into the extremely fitting condition of what was once called *servitore di campagna*[15]: a young man working for a landowner or sharecropper, receiving no salary but only food, the right to sleep in the hayloft or the stable, and some small seasonal perk. The character of Anguilla gives a new outlet to Pavese's issue of *work*: work might well be salvation, an allegory of moral engagement, but Anguilla, as a child, works without really being part of the world of work: he works without pay, and is given bread, board and work as a grace bestowed upon him. Later he will work in earnest, and make his fortune: not in his home village though, but in America; so the theme of real work will also be transferred to the remote and fabulous sphere of Pavese's America, the country of fortune for the rootless, rather than being set in the context

14 Anguilla, literally 'eel'. [Trans.]
15 Literally 'a country servant', roughly equivalent to a bondsman. [Trans.]

of the village or the city, within which it could perhaps be a means of salvation.

After making his fortune, Anguilla returns to his home village. Not by chance, Pavese here reprises a theme traditional throughout European literature in the first half of the twentieth century, from the stories of *déraciné* intellectuals returning only once to their childhood homes, to those of veterans going back to the homeland after the First or Second World War. By choosing this conventional theme, Pavese in fact intends to reach the narrative calmness we have mentioned, those places common to human experience through which the cry can be isolated and channelled back into purity, beyond any implications involving symbols or ciphered signs.

The village, swept over by the war, appears the same as ever, although 'not even one vine shoot had remained of the old ones, not even one head of cattle': 'strange how everything was changed and yet the same', 'everything had that smell, that taste, that colour it used to have back then'. Everything has changed, yet everything is the same. What determines this continuity? What does continuity consist of, and how much value does it have? The answer—which is the same for all these questions— is the dominant theme in *The Moon and the Bonfires*. Everything has changed but everything is the same because the village is dominated by death, and death allows things that look the same to take the place of dead things. The sons and daughters of the dead are almost like the dead; and above all, nature, far removed from her depleted human variants, allows today's vine shoots to be *the same* as yesterday's—through death.

When reading *The Moon and the Bonfires* one should bear in mind a fact of which Pavese was very much aware. The villages in the Langhe in which the narration is set register every month in their records episodes of suicide or self-destruction (like Valino's arson of his own farmhouse, with himself, his family and his cattle inside). One might say that these villages in particular, and especially a few families, are periodically and endemically visited by some form of death sickness. One village in the Langhe, Monforte, is known in the area as the 'village of the hanged', because several times a year some of its inhabitants choose that form of suicide; and it is striking that even a woman from abroad who had lived in the village for a while killed herself by the same method a few years ago.

For these reasons, the signs of death as a phenomenon or force warranting a 'dissimilar continuity' through time were recognized by Pavese as rooted in the very soil of the country. It is a sort of law, to which plants and animals submit more easily than men, if only because their offspring resembles them more closely.

It would be inaccurate to say that the signs of death (the burning down of Valino's farmhouse, the execution of Santa) are *foreshadowed* in the suffering of the motherless, fatherless child, who is alone, who cannot go to the festival because he has no shoes, who—when a little older—has to drive his master's daughters' coach. There is no foreshadowing, not least because death is never *foreshadowed* by suffering: it is something different. It is rather the desperate realization (especially in the evocations of childhood and adolescence) of being passively involved in a game that has death as its only reference point. This game causes suffering because it stops one having any roots, home, mother or father, love or country: it prevents one from owning or belonging, turns one into a mere thing through a wind change that is all the more sombre for being less stormy.

The supreme emblem of this destiny, ranking highest in Pavese's poetry, is the fate of Santa: the masters' daughter, beautiful and 'reckless' in a sense that encloses her whole being. Reckless because involved in a wartime political game double-crossing both the partisans and the Germans, a game already marked by death but at the same time representative of the fate of woman in that world, of the mutable choice, determined by a merciless rigour, made by one who *without meaning to* becomes a carrier and a victim of the 'feminine perception of infinity', as defined by Kierkegaard. It would be extremely superficial to see Santa's as the 'story of a spy' set at the time of the partisan war; but her crime, being a 'spy', is particularly revealing, because under the semblance of ambiguity or moral bewilderment in their historical sense it masks the stations of a rigorously unfolded destiny. Pavese's ultimate shrug (another one!) at the moment of Santa's execution, his mercilessly entrusting her 'to one who would take her into the next room and shoot at her', are traits of the behaviour of one who identifies with the victim and awaits an executioner. At the end of 1949, as Pavese is finishing *The Moon and the Bonfires*, Constance Dowling[16] returns to America. Pavese is left alone with what is inside Santa, which is

16 Constance Dowling (1920–69), an American model and actress who was close to Pavese during the time she spent in Italy between 1947 and 1950. [Trans.]

not solely himself, but cannot be wholly other than himself—unless at the time of an epiphany: the veiled tenderness with which Pavese has Santa's body burnt so that it cannot be violated is the descant to the apparent indifference with which Santa was delivered to her death. And this is Pavese's highest love poem—much higher than the faltering, often empty-ringing song of 'Death Will Come and Will Have Your Eyes'. But in the collection of that title we find two revealing verses, dated 4 April 1950:

> You are lying under the night
> like a locked dead horizon.

Here is the real key to *The Moon and the Bonfires*. Here, at the heart of the tradition of the great European novel, the human sacrifice warranting a 'dissimilar continuity' but not remedying solitude connects within the same existential experience the duty of death and the stunned, innocent, desperate realization of solitude before death, in death, after death. Thus in that collection of poems it is the first person plural that acquires the value of a moral revelation: the 'us', the 'with us' that does not break solitude but employs it as the face of an identification—an identification *first* in life, *then* in death:

> this death walking with us
> from morning to night, sleepless,
> heedless, like an old remorse,
> an absurd vice.[17]

---

17 Cesare Pavese, *Verrà la morte e avrà i tuoi occhi* (Turin: Einaudi, 1950) / *Disaffections: Complete Poems, 1930–1950* (Geoffrey Brock trans. and introd.) (Manchester: Carcanet 2004) [translation modified].

And here the experience of death, the obligation of death, are signs of guilt (the 'old remorse'), as is suicide ('vice'); but they are also *immoral* guarantees of the only alternative to solitude: the identification through which Pavese takes care of Santa's body. One and one is zero.

(From the letter 'to a girl', written from Bocca di Magra about a fortnight before the suicide):

> August 1950
>
> Dear Pierina,
>
> Can I tell you, love, that I have never woken up with a woman beside me who was mine, that the one I have loved never took me seriously, and that I've never known the grateful look in a woman's eyes when she gazes at a man? And can I remind you that, because of the work I've done, I've had constantly tense nerves and a sharp and ready fantasy, and a taste for sharing in other people's secrets? And that I've been in this world for forty-two years? One can't burn the candle at both ends—in my case I've burnt it all at one end only and the ash is the books I've written.
>
> [ . . . ]
>
> Love is like the grace of god—cunning is no use.
> As for me, I love you, Pierina, I love you *a bonfire*.

This is the sense in which I had spoken of a religion of death in Pavese. In this sense, the religion of death that I saw documented in Pavese's relationship with mythological images was set apart from the commonplaces of so-called decadentism, precisely because it sharply defined itself as a pessimistic religion of duty.

I have insisted on this misconstruction, not least because I think it is a sort of indicator relative to the reasons for the changing fortunes of the studies on Pavese and myth. These studies, as I have said, enjoyed a particularly fortunate moment roughly ten years ago, after which a sort of stagnation set in. Not that interest has waned—quite the opposite. Among the many essays on Pavese published over the last ten years, it is quite rare to find one that does not spend a number of pages on the problem of myth; and we have also on several occasions come across the theme of 'Pavese and myth' at the level of research done by university or even high-school students. My impression, however, is that the problem of Pavese's relationship with myth has been basically sidelined and turned into an occasion for more or less academic exercises. During the current decade, a few fine works on Pavese's *oeuvre* or on some of its fundamental aspects have offered pages on the problem of myth that, while better informed than the ones written twenty years ago, can hardly be accused of excess originality.

I believe that the special fortune enjoyed ten years ago by studies on Pavese and myth was mainly due to the following reasons. On the one hand, those studies did mark the definite appearance onto the Italian scene of critical instruments connected to the so-called human sciences, and especially to cultural anthropology. This was in itself a novelty, it was attractive, *à la page* even. It was something that tended to allay the guilt within Italian culture, more or less secretly afflicted as it was by an often quite justified 'provincialism complex'. But aside from this more superficial aspect, which nonetheless did have a certain weight, it seems to me that those studies were seen back then as an instrument apt to release Pavese's figure from the label of 'decadent poet' without sacrificing some of the objective and visibly important aspects of his *oeuvre*—apt, in other words, to grant moral legitimacy to those features in Pavese's work that might most readily be labelled as 'decadent'. Those who were aware of the moral rigour in Pavese's work—a rigour judged quite limited by those who read his work as decadent—were offered the chance to score a victory on their opponents' ground: to show them that Pavese, exactly where he had been closest to 'decadent' positions, exactly on the ground of myth, of the science of myth, of his presumed irrationalist complacency—exactly there, Pavese had not been in the least 'decadent'. Or, as we might want to say: at the moment of greatest temptation, virtue stood revealed.

I said earlier that in the unfolding of criticism relative to a certain author one should look for the interaction between the components of his work and the historical and cultural situation of his critics. One should, therefore, ask which and how many elements in Pavese's *oeuvre* have intervened to create this situation and interact with our situation.

Here I can only add a few observations, of relative value, since I myself, as one of the parties involved, probably lack the objectivity necessary to delve any deeper. My impression is—and once again I stress the words 'my impression is', for it is difficult to offer more than 'impressions' in any discourse taking place only *dix ans plus tard* on vicissitudes in which we are personally involved—my impression is that Pavese played a great part in the stalling of the studies on his relationship with myth, since he himself lived in advance through several aspects of the cultural phase in which we find ourselves, and set out their presence in his works with an authority we cannot easily elude. The problem of moral evaluation, the confrontation with so-called decadentism: Pavese lived through these things with extreme involvement, if not without irony, much earlier than we did. Mostly, it is him who pushes us to consider these things essential, insofar as he has predicted and pre-lived, and also contributed to, a phase of Italian culture in which the problem of the moral qualities of a work of art is shown as not easily separated from the problem posed by other qualities. With the difference that he was able to make use of the creative possibilities of such a phase, whereas I don't know to which extent we might be able to. As for the problem of critical instruments, of the recourse to methodologies matured within the scope of the so-called human sciences: these also were pressing problems for Pavese, who certainly was not a specialist either in ethnology or in the science of myth, but had a much better grasp of these disciplines and of their relationships with culture as a whole, and with literature in particular, than many of his posthumous critics. I am not saying that Pavese had a clear view of the connections and contrasts between the works of ethnology, science of myth and deep psychology that he read and promoted for publication—rather, that

in a very real sense he pre-lived the raging of methodological questions I have mentioned (albeit in the form
of concerns that back then, in the language of Italy back
then, he would call concerns about 'poetics'). And in this
too, he plays a part in blocking us. He experienced what
would happen too deeply for us to find it easy, living as
we are in his pre-lived future, not to draw back into it as
we concern ourselves with him.

# R. M. Rilke, *Duino Elegies*
## EDITOR'S NOTE

As shown by unpublished documents, Jesi began to translate the *Duino Elegies*[1] in 1959. Since that time, he would be in constant dialogue with Rilke: we recall his 1964 essay *Rilke e l'Egitto*, later collected with other Rilkean essays in *Letteratura e mito*; the pages he wrote in *Germania segreta*;[2] his monograph *Rilke*;[3] his editing and translation of *The Notebooks of Malte Laurids Brigge*;[4] and, finally, *Esoterismo e linguaggio mitologico. Studi su Rainer Maria Rilke*, VOL. 1[5] and its (sadly unfinished) sequel, *Traduzione e duplicità dei linguaggi* [Translation and Duplicity in Languages].

Probably written soon after *Esoterismo e linguaggio mitologico*, the following essay was meant as an introduction for a Garzanti edition of the Elegies (the original typescript is subtitled 'With an Introductory Note by F. Jesi' and includes 'Notes to the Editors' in line with the house style adopted for the 'I Grandi Libri' series and quoting, as additional material, the note Jesi had appended to his translation of the *Malte*).

As he had done in his 'Reading of Rimbaud's "Bateau ivre"', Jesi recalls Heidegger's famous essay 'What Are Poets

---

1 Rainer Maria Rilke, *Duineser Elegien* (Leipzig: Insel Verlag, 1923). [Trans.]

2 Furio Jesi, *Germania segreta: miti nella cultura tedesca del '900* (Milan: Silva, 1967) / *Secret Germany: Myth in Twentieth-Century German Culture* (Richard Braude trans.) (London: Seagull Books, 2020).

3 Furio Jesi, *Rilke* (Florence: La Nuova Italia, 1971).

4 Rainer Maria Rilke, *I quaderni di Malte Laurids Brigge* (Furio Jesi trans.) (Milan: Garzanti, 1974) / *The Notebooks of Malte Laurids Brigge* (Burton Pike trans.) (Champaign, IL: Dalkey Archive, 2008).

5 Furio Jesi, *Esoterismo e linguaggio mitologico* (Messina: G. D'Anna, 1976).

For?' (*Wozu Dichter?*),[6] that he had elsewhere described as a discourse held first and foremost *with* Rilke, albeit outwardly about Hölderlin. But above all, as the 'Reading' had done, this essay sets out, in its final configuration, the theme of the 'commonplaces'. Here, however, the *topoi* of Rilke's poetics are separated and left to settle, depositing each of their 'contents' in the *Sonnets to Orpheus*[7] so as to become pure asemantic entities ringing 'empty' within the text of the Elegies. Thus, freeing them from any symbolic, doctrinal or esoteric interpretation, Jesi reads the Elegies as an experiment performed by Rilke so that the word would vibrate only with the naked will to speak. The architecture of phonemes that no longer say anything is set at the point of intersection between historical time and unfathomable secret, between existence and non-existence.

This essay was first published under the title 'R. M. Rilke, *Elegie di Duino*. Scheda introduttiva di Furio Jesi' in *Cultura tedesca* 12 (December 1999): 111–20.

---

6 Martin Heidegger delivered this essay as a lecture at a commemorative meeting of Rainer Maria Rilke's twentieth death anniversary in 1946. It was later published in his anthology *Holzwege* (Frankfurt am Main: Vittorio Klostermann, 1950) / 'What Are Poets For?' in Martin Heidegger, *Poetry, Language, Thought* (Albert Hofstadter trans.) (New York: Harper and Row, 1975), pp. 91–142]. [Trans.]

7 Rainer Maria Rilke, *Die Sonette an Orpheus* (Leipzig: Insel-Verlag, 1923) / *Sonnets to Orpheus with Letters to a Young Poet* (Stephen Cohn trans.) (Manchester: Carcanet, 2000)]. [Trans.]

# R. M. Rilke, *Duino Elegies*

## INTERPRETATIONS OF THE ELEGIES

Among Rilke's works, the *Duineser Elegien* (together with
the *Sonette an Orpheus*) have for many years drawn special
attention from a strand of criticism seeking to find in the
poet's pages some 'words of eternal wisdom' (as C. J.
Burckhardt ironically wrote to H. von Hofmannsthal in
1920, when the Elegies were still in progress)[1]. No less than
a sacred text for Rilke worshippers, a text that would be
grotesquely celebrated by some cultured Nazis (Gottfried
Benn recalls how in November 1943 the journal of the
Reich's navy lauded the Elegies as the work in which
Rilke had, 'in his own way, outlined the new times'), the
*Duineser Elegien* have been the subject of much reflection
among philosophers (a wide range of examples can be
found in Heftrich):[2] best known and very much followed
is Heidegger's essay 'Wozu Dichter?', although in fact
only the VIII and IX Elegies are directly quoted there.
While not neglecting the components related to ideology,
poetics and 'religion' in the Elegies, critical discourse
takes on a more strictly literary character in a work such

---

1 Carl Jacob Burckhardt, *Carl Jacob Burckhardt zu Hugo von Hofmannsthal*
(Frankfurt am Main: S. Fischer Verlag, 1974). [Trans.]
2 Eckhard Heftrich, *Die Philosophie und Rilke* (Freiburg: K. Alber, 1962)

as Rehm's *Orpheus*[3], which even from its subtitle draws attention to the religion 'of the dead' or 'of death' as documented in the Elegies. And as early as 1941, Beissner had in fact subjected the Elegies to an exquisitely historico-literary investigation within the purview of his *Geschichte*.[4] This privileged character of the Elegies in the context of Rilke's *oeuvre*, in many ways legitimate—albeit privileged as the gospel of a doctrine, which is less legitimate—has turned into a taint on them during the last twenty years owing to the heavy devaluation of Rilke in large sectors of criticism (and not only Marxist criticism). In a 1943 essay, later published in his *Letture di poeti*,[5] Croce had defined the Elegies a 'didactic poem', and even Errante, in the first version of his book on Rilke, had attacked the Elegies and Sonnets (though he did retract that later) for not too dissimilar a reason: a 'poet-poet' must resist the temptation to turn philosopher.[6] In more recent works by Rilke scholars (such as Fülleborn, Destro, Himmel, etc.), the methodological problem of an approach to the Elegies is reconsidered beyond these constraints (which are not however devoid of an objective foundation), and set out mainly in terms of a precise philological analysis of the text as the document of a poetics. As is in fact the case with each one of Rilke's works, here too another extremely difficult problem

---

3 Walther Rehm, *Orpheus: der Dichter und die Toten, Selbstdeutung und Totenkult bei Novalis-Hölderlin-Rilke* (Düsseldorf: L. Schwann Verlag, 1950).

4 Friedrich Beissner, *Geschichte der deutschen Elegien* (Berlin: De Gruyter Mouton, 1965)

5 Benedetto Croce, *Letture di poeti e riflessioni sulla teoria e la critica della poesia* (Bari: Laterza, 1950). [Trans.]

6 Vincenzo Errante, *Rilke. Storia di un'anima e di una poesia* (Milan: Alpes, 1930). [Trans.]

stems from the very fragmented and ambiguous character of the documentary materials available (suffice it to say that, particularly in the case of the Elegies, the Zinn edition[7] cannot be considered a true critical edition).

## THE ELEGIES

### *The Text: Time, Place and Modalities of Composition*

The text of the *Duineser Elegien* that Rilke sent in 1922 to his publisher, Anton Kippenberg, proprietor of Insel Verlag, is in a strict sense the result of work done in Muzot roughly during the first twenty days of February of that year, when he also composed the *Sonette an Orpheus*. To give the most superficial description of his work in those days, we might say that he re-examined a large quantity of verses written several years earlier, discarding some and writing some new ones that in some cases replaced those he had expunged. The lack or ambiguity of materials on which Rilkean philology can be brought to bear makes it difficult to precisely establish the timeline followed by the poet to arrive at the final text: if this is true of any of Rilke's works, it is all the more so in this case. We are meant to reconstruct the phases of work concentrated in the span of a few days, the progression of possibly important decisions and rethinkings that may have happened overnight in the brief course of three weeks at most, on the basis of old and new, doubtlessly incomplete autograph documents. There are however some certain, or almost certain, elements by which we can distinguish at least between the earlier passages of the Elegies and those composed later in February 1922. On the basis of

---

7 Rainer Maria Rilke, *Sämtliche Werke*, 6 VOLS (Ernst Zinn ed.) (Leipzig: Insel Verlag, 1955–66). [Trans.]

the indications given by the poet in his letters, as well as study of the manuscripts that have survived (or are accessible to scholars), we may assume that Rilke wrote Elegies I and II, plus some parts (perhaps only the beginning, certainly at least the beginning) of the III, VI, IX and X, in the castle of Duino during January–February 1912; part of the VI in January–February 1913 at Ronda in Spain; what was still missing from the III and further passages of the VI in the autumn of 1913 in Paris; and the IV in November 1915 in Munich. Before 1922, Rilke also wrote other passages of the Elegies, later expunged during preparation of the final text, that he had meant to include under 'the heading of "Fragmentary Pieces" which, as the second part of the book of Elegies, will contain all that is contemporaneous to them—what time, so to speak, demolished before it was brought forth or has so cut off in its development that it displays broken surfaces' (letter to L. Andreas Salomé, dated 19 February 1922).[8] Some of these passages were certainly replaced with new ones: the central section of a first version of the X, and a whole V that made way for the V of the final text, added 'in a radiant after-storm' after Rilke had already announced the completion of the cycle to at least three of his correspondents. In February 1922, Rilke thus seems to have written for the first time both the VII and VIII, plus some passages meant to integrate the existing text and—after about a week's break—the whole V as found in the final text.

---

8 See Rainer Maria Rilke, *Letters of Rainer Maria Rilke, 1910–1926* (Jane Bannard Greene and M. D. Herter Norton trans) (London: Norton, 1969). [Trans.]

From a first analysis, this seems to show how, before setting to work on the conclusion of the Elegies in February 1922, Rilke in fact already had roughly half (about four hundred?), if not a much larger number, of the approximately eight hundred and fifty verses that would form the final text. He also had a sort of general outline of the work, set out in 1912: when still at Duino he had established that he would write ten elegies, and composed, among other things, the openings for several, which remained part of the final text—even (and this is certain) the beginning of the X, the last one, whose first twelve verses he kept unchanged. We do not however know to what extent this outline really was, as it would seem, a detailed plan; and we are even less clear about the extent to which this possible plan may have been followed in 1922. Neither can basic quantitative information (about half of the verses might have been already composed) in itself shed much light on the modalities of the operation that, in February 1922, resulted in the final text.

## Genesis and Completion of the Elegies (and Sonnets), as Related by Rilke

In his verbal and written colloquies with Princess Taxis, Rilke gave a precise account—precise, that is, as to the minutiae of detail—of the first origin of the Elegies. In January 1912, he was alone in the castle at Duino; one day he received a business letter, and in order to reflect on the tone of his reply he went for a walk along the castle ramparts, sheer above the sea. There, as a windstorm was raging, he heard a voice exclaim the words that would become the first verse of Elegy I: '*Wer, wenn ich schrie,*

*hörte mich denn aus der Engel Ordnungen?*"⁹ Some other
verses rang out in the same way: he took note of them,
registering them passively; but later on the same day he
was seized by a creative impetus surging forth from
his having experienced that mysterious voice, and by
nightfall the full text of the First Elegy (which remained
identical in the final arrangement of the cycle) had
been completed. This *motus animi continuus* also produced within a short time the text of the Second Elegy
and subsequently the beginning of some others, including
the Tenth. Rilke does not, and in fact never will, directly
state whose voice he thought had dictated to him the
opening of the Elegies. Some hints might lead us to
believe he might have been thinking of a 'divine' or
'angelic' voice: but with Rilke, these adjectives are always
quite ambi-guous. Which divinity? Which angel? A hint
found in the letter to Witold Hulewicz (13 November
1925)— 'The "angel" of the Elegies has nothing to do
with the angel of the Christian heaven (rather with the
angel figures of Islam)'¹⁰—might lead us to surmise, at
least at one stage of Rilke's reflection on his own work
(whether as early as 1912, or in 1922, or later, after completion, we do not know), the intervention of the fascinating Islamic image of the immense archangel Gabriel,
filling the skies with his form and transmitting the
doctrine of the Quran to Mohammed. If, for the moment,
we step back from the search for the identity (in the
Rilkean mythological context) of the voice heard at
Duino, we can observe that this version of the birth of

9 In David Oswald's translation: 'Who, if I cried out, would hear me
then, out of the orders of angels?'—see *Duino Elegies*, p. 27. [Trans.]
10 Rainer Maria Rilke, *Briefe aus Muzot: 1921 bis 1926* (Leipzig: Insel,
1937), p. 33 / *Letters of Rainer Maria Rilke, 1910–1926*.

the Elegies is a commonplace characteristic of the poet's autobiographical declarations: much earlier, *Cornet*[11] had been 'the unforeseen gift of a single night' (letter to Hermann Pongs, 17 August 1924), and the identification of the operation of composition with nothing less than mediumistic writing is meant to have occurred with the *Nachlass*,[12] which Rilke stated was his work not as a poet but merely as a scrivener, subjected to the presence and almost to the dictation of a dead man, Count C.W. If, however, we examine the letters by which Rilke, in February 1922, immediately announced the completion of the Elegies to A. Kippenberg, to Princess Taxis and to L. Andreas Salomé, we realize that this commonplace does recur, but is altered by a slightly different tone. True, Rilke says: 'All in a few days. It was a nameless storm, a hurricane in the spirit (like that time in Duino), all that was fibre in me and fabric cracked, eating was not to be thought of, God knows who fed me' (letter to Princess Taxis, 11 February 1922; almost the same words in the letter written on the same day to L. Andreas Salomé). Yet he insists on stressing not that the new passages of the Elegies were dictated to him, but rather that he was allowed to resist until completion, 'to survive up to this' (in the letter quoted to L. Andreas Salomé, the German original lays even stronger emphasis on the '*I* was allowed': *ich habe überstehen dürfen*), and that he had

---

11 Reference to Rainer Maria Rilke, *Die Weise von Liebe und Tod des Cornets Christoph Rilke* (Leipzig: Insel Verlag, 1899) / *The Love and Death of Cornet Christopher Rilke*; Bilingual EDN (Stephen Mitchell trans.) (San Francisco: Arion Press, 1983). [Trans.]

12 Rainer Maria Rilke, *Aus den Nachlass der Grafen C.W.* (Leipzig: Insel Verlag, 1950) / *From the Remains of Count C.W.*, Bilingual EDN (J. B. Leishman trans.) (London: Hogarth Press, 1952). [Trans.]

been 'equal to the task, right through everything' (letter quoted to Princess Taxis). The general context in which Rilke sets the events of February 1922, like the one framing the initial steps at Duino in 1912, doubtlessly also implies a certain submission of the poet to the 'hurricane', the 'storm' unleashed around him; but if at Duino this was presented first and foremost as passive, in Muzot it has been transfigured into the power to 'survive', to hold out. To begin with, when referring to the operation that led to the completion of the Elegies, Rilke does not use the formula 'I was given them', but rather 'I was allowed to survive'. All the more significant, then, to find that same formula of the 'given' poem referring to the *Sonette an Orpheus*, also composed in early February 1922. In sending the text to Gertrud Ouckama Knoop, mother of Wera, the dead girl to whom the Sonnets are a 'Memorial', Rilke writes: 'In a few days of spontaneous emotion, when I actually intended to take up some other work, these Sonnets were given [*geschenkt*] to me' (letter dated 7 February 1922). The contrast is sharp: Rilke consciously intended to set to work on something specific and different (*an anderes heranzuge-hen*), namely, the completion of the Elegies, but in the meantime, independent of his will, the Sonnets were 'given' (*geschenkt*) to him. In the letter to Hulewicz, he will confirm the same vision, the same relationship between deliberate work on the one hand, and almost passively received 'gift' on the other: 'the new Elegies and their conclusion were preceded, in just a few days, by the *Sonette an Orpheus*, which imposed themselves tempestuously (and which had *not* been in my plan)'.

The completion of the Elegies was thus the deliberate actualization of a 'project' or 'plan' ('*in meinem Plane*'); not so the composition of the Sonnets. Let it be clear that we have so far not expressed *our* opinion, but only sought to understand Rilke's attitude (partly altered between 1912 and 1922) as he spoke of the genesis and completion of the Elegies and Sonnets.

## A CRITICAL APPROACH
## TO THE TEXT OF THE ELEGIES AND SONNETS

It is almost stating the obvious to say that the means at our disposal for an analysis of Rilke's texts do not help us to approach—let alone solve—the problem of the objectivity of the mysterious experiences hinted at by Rilke. There is a break in continuity between our perception of reality and Rilke's occultism, which we can therefore only examine from the outside. We might however be able to examine Rilke's esotericism from the inside, by configuring it as the general position in which the poet, when connecting to a secret, places himself with regard to his readers, who also share in a secret by way of their connection with him. From this point of view, we might legitimately formulate a few hypotheses and 'models' of the modalities of our approach to the text of the *Duineser Elegien* and its genesis—such modalities not being entirely gratuitous, because inherent to the historicization of the poet's experience, and thus stemming from the interaction between our knowledge and the extent to which Rilke is historicizable. From this same point of view, we might therefore say that the *Duineser Elegien* correspond to one of the last phases of the process of reification lived through by Rilke—or, in other words, of his journey towards the condition of 'blind and pure instrument' of the unknowable that must use the poet, cause the poet to write, even cause the poet to 'be written' if he truly wants to be himself: 'But a day will come when my hand will be far from me, and if I bid it write, it will write words I do not intend. [ . . . ] this time I shall be written'.[13] This separation of the hand (no longer obeying) from the poet is matched by another passage in the *Malte*. Having slid under the table to look for a pencil he had dropped, the very young Malte sees his own hand in the penumbra and 'coming out of the wall [ . . . ], a bigger, uncommonly skinny hand of a kind I had never seen. It was searching around in similar fashion from the other side, and both outstretched hands were blindly moving towards each other. [ . . . ] I felt that one of those hands belonged to me and that it was letting itself into something irreparable'.

The child pulls back and breaks contact with the spectral hand. But—as Rilke said himself—the *Malte* is a 'mould': the *Duineser Elegien* were the cast within that mould, the hand of the adult Malte / Rilke being first forced to make contact with the spectral hand at Duino in 1912, and Rilke deciding later (at Muzot in 1922) to have his own will coincide with that delving into the 'irreparable'. In Rilke's mythological language, the cycle of the Elegies is announced, at the moment of completion, as one of his own limbs, finally whole and functioning, by his choice, after a long time: since 1912, when he had painfully perceived its intimation and its pressing

---

13 Rilke, *I quaderni di Malte Laurids Brigge / The Notebooks of Malte Laurids Brigge* [translation modified]. [Trans.]

towards actualization. When Rilke, having completed the Elegies at six o'clock on the evening of 11 February 1922, writes to Princess Taxis: 'from this [the last Elegy] my hand is still trembling', he implicitly declares that he has finally acquired a hand, and, in full awareness, has ordered his hand to delve into the 'irreparable'. He will write to L. Andreas Salomé: 'Now I *know myself again—* it really had been a mutilation of my heart, that the Elegies were not here'.

We might at this point ask whether it makes any sense to speak of the 'content' of the Elegies. The question may appear paradoxical, for the presence in the Elegies of a vast abundance of symbolic materials from the most diverse origins may at first give the impression that such materials were more or less clearly ordained into a hugely complicated doctrinal architecture, and that in fact the Elegies should be read as a very outspoken essay in metaphysical-didactic poetry, a sort of *sui generis* philosophy in verse. If we also choose to dwell on the fact that many of those symbolic materials are recurring *topoi* in Rilke's previous production, and that each of them may be reconnected to a doctrinal attitude, we are faced with the picture of a didactic poem, a final and self-vindicating work in which Rilke is meant to have gathered the *summa* of his doctrine so as to display its fullness, consistency and legitimacy. If, however, we place the *Duineser Elegien* within the perspective of a journey towards the condition of 'blind and pure instrument', we realize that the best way of reading them without *a priori* missing their tensions is seeing them as purely the *summa* of rhetorical (in the widest sense of the word) occasions, keeping the poet's speech this side of the silence to which it would be destined in the ultimate phase of reification, when reduced to a 'blind, pure'—and *mute*—'instrument'. The contrast itself, perceivable in Rilke's attitude when he describes the completion of the Elegies as the outcome of a deliberate plan and the creation of the Sonnets as an unforeseen 'gift', can clarify the modalities of this enduring of the poet's voice on this side of the 'soundless fate' (Elegy X, verse 105) into which the dead youth must venture. The Rilke operating at Muzot in 1922 is a poet fully aware by now of his own inability to become a 'blind and pure instrument' completely free of any debris of conscious volition. The frustration of the possessive will (imposed or, if we like, justified by the purpose of perfect reification) is metamorphosed: since it is not possible to free oneself from the final debris of volition and to become a pure object unaware of any will, the fault is redressed by being turned into a privilege. The journey ends (Rilke *wants* the journey to end: he *wants* to complete the Elegies): hence, in this final phase, the poet who is aware of being a poet declares himself a 'blind and pure instrument' of the unknowable, of the secret, to the point that even the inalienable debris of his will coincides with the will of the unknowable. The poet *wants* to speak— hence what speaks in him is the unknowable. But the speech ringing out no longer has any content: it is pure will to speak. The content of the secret's voice ringing out at last is simply the fact that 'the secret speaks'. For this to happen, the modalities of speech need to be puri- fied of all content, in such total terms as to enclose in one point all past activity, all words ever uttered. Hence the organization, in the context of the Elegies, of the multitude of Rilkean commonplaces, including the oldest—but also the need for some place into which the contents of those *topoi* can be channelled, so that in the Elegies they may ring hollow, as pure rhetorical occasions. The *Sonette an Orpheus*, the 'given', unplanned work overriding the completion of the Elegies, are precisely that: the place where the contents of Rilkean *topoi* flow for the last time (and once and for all), so that those same *topoi* may ring hollow in the Elegies. In that place, they appear estranged from the speech of the poet who has staked his last card on the coincidence between his will and the will of the unknowable, because they are found in the context of a work that, in Rilke's mythological language, is 'given', not willed. Several scholars, as if almost hypnotized by the presence of Orpheus, have failed to realize that in fact a tension is at work in the Sonnets between Orpheus and the mythological figure of a dead girl (Wera Ouckama Knoop, for whom, as we have seen, the Sonnets are a 'Memorial')—a *kore*, in the language of Greek mythology—and that this tension implies the victory of the *kore* over Orpheus, as with Orpheus being torn apart by the Maenads and 'vanquished' by Eurydice herself, who fades away into the underworld without him. If Orpheus is the poet of a poetry endowed with content, spellbinding and celebratory because it tells and celebrates the truth, the *kore* is the personification of a poetry that is purely the rhetorical occasion of not being silent, because one cannot be totally silent—that is, because the poet cannot fully become an object. The dead girl, the *kore*, prevailing over Orpheus in the Sonnets, is the dead girl, the *kore*, the Lament (*Klage*) in the Elegies: she is *the elegy*, the lament with no content other than the deliberate choice of not being silent, since it is not possible to be at the same time a living poet and a mute (as well as 'blind and pure') instrument of the unknowable.

This sort of approach to the text of the Elegies thus implies that any research focusing on the apparently symbolic formulations supposedly articulating, within the architecture of the cycle, a presumed doctrinal, philosophical, esoteric or anthropological apparatus should be seen as very secondary, perhaps even misleading. Clearly, these formulae and this architecture must be studied, but not so much as details of *maisons philosophales* or stone grimoires of alchemical doctrines—rather, as rhetorical occasions which, when ritualized, hold the poet back on this side of silence. Think, for example, of the differential semantic values of adjectives such as *entsetzlich* ('horrible'?) and *schrecklich* ('terrible'? 'terrifying'?), delimiting each other within the enclosed field of the Elegies. When used as a noun, 'the Terrible' (or 'the Terrifying') is presented as early as the opening of Elegy I as a primary occasion for speech, as a cry, and in Elegy III makes way for 'the Horrible', in an extremely complex game of tonalities and apparent articulations of the cry, which at times is pushed to the limits of the colloquial expression only to be drastically brought back to the exclamation, the single phoneme. Consider also how, in Elegies VII and VIII, the practice of the cry becomes a reflection on the cry, the cry folding back onto itself until it becomes 'Natur' (almost as in a famous notation recurring in Gustav

Mahler: *'wie ein Naturlaut'*—'like a sound of nature', 'like a voice of nature'). Considerations such as these could be multiplied over hundreds of pages, which undoubtedly would highlight the dexterity (and the broad-minded use of stylistic means) of that architectural composition and its carefully planned, extremely complex outcomes, elaborate as can be and calculated to the smallest detail. Suffice it to note, on the one hand, the discouraging complications of the metrical scheme, continually altered under the guise of uniform sound, and on the other, the acrobatic articulations of morphemes connected to *sein* ('to be'), the verb infinitives often used as nouns, such as *Dasein*, *da Sein*, *Hiersein*, or also *Dastehen*, etc. It is quite doubtful that such tightrope walking should be seen as proof of Rilke's trust in the 'earned word' (Elegy IX, verse 30) as a vector of meaning, rather than as an avowal of the asemantic nucleus of the word. True, in the Ninth Elegy Rilke points to that 'earned word', which might be identified with *ein Menschliches*—'a human[ness]' (Elegy II, verses 74–5); but it also seems clear that this hint should be juxtaposed to the imminent access, in the Tenth, to the 'soundless fate', the dead youth's journey without return. Rilke seems to be drawing back from that threshold, but then closes with a masked quote from the Bible (Joel II, 23) on the motif of springtime rain drenching the 'dark earth', exactly as music-lament had penetrated the 'parched numbness' at the end of Elegy I. This circularity (the cycle of water rising from the earth and falling back into it) in the two underlined words of the last four verses in Elegy X (*steigendes*, 'rising'; *fällt*, 'it falls'), is the circularity of a speech that 'says' nothing, but only 'resonates'. Thus in Rilke's mythology the cycle of water is the rhythm of the secret side by side with the flowing of historical time, and the vicissitude of water eternally 'rising' and 'fall[ing]' *says* nothing of what happens in earthly history, even though its sound echoes throughout it.

# On an Early Writing by Lukács

EDITOR'S NOTE

The following essay was first published in *Nuova corrente* 71 (1976), together with a translation by Jesi and Giuseppe Sertoli of the dialogue 'Von der Armut am Geiste' ('On Poverty of Spirit'), written by György Lukács after the suicide of Irma Seidler. Jesi sheds light on the connections between the dialogue and the book *Soul and Form* (dedicated by Lukács to his friend's memory), harking back to the famous pages on the relationship between Kierkegaard and Regine Olsen and reprising some of the themes present in his own *Kierkegaard*, especially in the chapter 'The Demonic. Aesthetics and Eschatology'. The complex didactics and rituals in Kierkegaard are however overridden by the dimension ('adolescent-like' and 'extraneous to real existence') in which Lukács's text situates Irma's actual suicide.

Agnes Heller once wrote that her teacher, Lukács, 'integrated his love into his work, and this was his tragedy. *But he integrated this tragedy with his life*'.[1] Jesi's essay, on the other hand, sees the 'non-correspondence between literary work and life' as the breach giving Lukács a way out of the adolescent 'age' (the only 'space reserved by bourgeois culture to the practice of poetry') and into mature life, a life made of 'years' and of power.

The connection with the essay on Pavese is very close: when poetry (the relationship with myth) remains suspended in an *age-adolescence*, the *religio mortis* rules as a religion of

---

1 From Heller's essay, 'Georg Lukács and Irma Seidler' [1979] in Agnes Heller (ed.), *Lukács Reappraised* (New York: Columbia University Press, 1983), pp 27–62. [Trans.]

solitary sacrifice; while the vital destruction of the self, a destruction without sacrifice 'in which the lover is nullified *in* his beloved (not *in front* of his beloved)', is precluded.

## On an Early Writing by Lukács

The impression one gets today while reading Lukács's 'On Poverty of Spirit'[1] is that of a tonality of discourse, a state of mind, affects and habitual behaviours for which the only appropriate qualifier would be: adolescent-like. One struggles to express this differently, while being aware of saying something correct, albeit in a rough form. Not so much for that qualifier, 'adolescent-like'; but 'tonality of discourse', 'state of mind', 'affects', 'habitual behaviours'—look at these expressions on the page after enclosing them in quotation marks: there's nothing worse. They take their positions, *bien figées*, not hardened but, worse still, unwittingly charged with an outrageous assuredness, about a text that would require something entirely different—more sympathy, perhaps.

> I have almost entirely forgotten my neighbour. I see that it was not real sympathy I had for him. Downstairs, on my way out, I sometimes ask whether any news has come from him, and what news. And I am happy when it is good. But I exaggerate. I really have no need to know. That

---

1 Georg Lukács, 'On Poverty of Spirit' in *Soul and Form* (John T. Sanders and Katie Terezakis eds, Anna Bostock trans.) (New York; Chichester: Columbia University Press, 2009), translation modified. [Trans.]

I sometimes feel a sudden impulse to walk into
the next room has nothing to do with him.[2]

That text demands sympathy while at the same time
refusing it, and thus reveals itself as adolescent-like.
Writing pages like these on the occasion of an actual
suicide, creating a fictional dialogue of this sort between
two apparently discordant voices that in fact harmonize
from the outset in the author's mind, on subjects like life
and death, 'living without life', the artist vs. the 'normal'
person (i.e. a person who is not an artist, but thus possesses 'the living life' rather than 'ordinary life', dead
life)—this means asking for sympathy and at the same
time rejecting it: putting oneself at the centre of attention,
but within a space enclosed by transparent and impenetrable walls which others are destined to always see as the
next room. And it means talking to oneself, convinced
that one can listen to oneself because in any case one is
also thinking of something more besides, convinced that
the dialogue with oneself is always with reservations, and
that it counts when it is not uttered (as opposed to dialogue with others, in which only what they hear does in
fact count). The author of this dialogue is not necessarily
the artist, but it is certain that others only seldom are
'normal people' in the sense seen above. This adjective,
'normal' (which is not the same as 'ordinary'), is always
in the air, but never uttered; rather, only alluded to by the
mask of normality that is the quietness of the male protagonist while he speaks 'calmly, simply'. The adjective
'normal' cannot be uttered in the dialogue because it is
what the prevalently absent person in the dialogue—the

---

2 Quoted from Rilke, *I quaderni di Malte Laurids Brigge* [*The Notebooks
of Malte Laurids Brigge* [translation modified].

suicide woman—could not be: neither 'normal', nor an artist. And the dialogue *is* the absent person; the dialogue precisely is the suicide woman: it is made from her, out of her, just like the building is the foreman's wife, sacrificed so that the building could be erected ('She had to die, so that my work could be completed, so that nothing should remain for me in the world but my work'). The suicide woman could not be either 'normal' or an artist; the word *normal* cannot therefore be uttered: others are not said to be 'normal', but rather defined as those who 'live without life'. The suicide woman cannot give to the work what she could not be; yet she has become the work, and one can therefore speak of the work—in fact, it is the work that can in this way speak of itself as it is now. There is much of Kierkegaard in all this: his sermon 'The Work of Love in Recollecting One Who Is Dead',[3] but with its fundamental premises reversed, and perhaps rightly so, in line with Kierkegaard's intention. In Kierkegaard's words, 'the dead one has nothing to pay us back with [for the memory]': a statement that remains paradoxically true when translated into: the dead person has nothing to repay us for memory, since he has lost everything by giving himself to us as the substance of the act of remembering him with love. In this sense, the separation inflicted by Kierkegaard on Regine Olsen is the ritual equivalent of a suicide forced on her (or of the realization, on Kierkegaard's part, of the fact that 'something', 'something

---

3 In the collection of 'sermons': *Kjerlighedens gjerninger: Nogle christelige overveielser i talers form* (Copenhagen: C.A. Reitzel, 1847) / Søren Kierkegaard, 'The Work of Love in Recollecting One Who Is Dead' in *Works of Love*, VOL. 2.9 (Howard V. Hong and Edna H. Hong eds and trans) (Princeton, NJ: Princeton University Press, 1995), pp. 345–58. [Trans.]

frightening', has played a trick on himself and Regine, ineluctably forcing the ritual equivalent of suicide on her, and the ritual equivalent of survival on him);[4] and in Lukács's pages, the suicide of Irma Seidler is identified with Kierkegaard's ritual in respect of Regine. In Lukács, the suicide woman could not be an artist; but she was the artist's victim, and therefore—in the dialogue—one can speak of him, albeit only with the gloomy eloquence appropriate to one who lives 'without life' as 'ordinary' people do—but who, unlike them, lives without life 'consciously and with clarity', or at least attempts to do so: the subsequent suicide of the male character in the dialogue—not of Lukács—seems to show the failure of this attempt, but on a different level than that of Lukács's actual, physical existence. And this different level seems to be that of the adolescent-like dimension of existence, which is basically extraneous to the modalities of actual, physical existence: almost a temporary participation of that actual existence in a foreign universe.

As collections of letters and memoirs would lead us to at least suspect,[5] dialogues like the one composed by Lukács probably did in fact happen, early in the century and perhaps also later, not between adolescents, but between intellectuals or artists who might well have been in their thirties. In the Mitteleuropean milieu, for one, it

---

4 See Jesi, *Kierkegaard*.

5 I shall only quote, by way of an example, two collections of materials that, respectively in an indirect and a direct manner, are connected with Rilke: P. Modersohn-Becker, *Briefe und Tagebuchblätter, herausgegeben und biographisch eingeführt von S.D. Gallwitz* (Munich: Wolff, 1925); and M. von Hattinberg, *Rilke e Benvenuta*, (E. Müller trans., R. Paoli introd.) (Florence: Sansoni, 1949) / *Rilke and Benvenuta: A Book of Thanks* (Cyrus Brooks trans.) (London: William Heinemann, 1949).

seems as if the artists and intellectuals of those years, between late nineteenth and early twentieth century, only reached a true adolescent-like tonality at what should be the adult age of thirty or later, at the end of a protracted childhood made of erudite imitations and onslaughts of a precocious maturity that remained the maturity of the *enfant prodige*—and, once reached that state, they recognized it as a safe haven in which it would be desirable or even fateful to remain forever. 'I never grow out of adolescence', Mann wrote to his brother at the age of twenty-six.[6] The relationship between Lukács's piece and the dialogue of Tonio Kröger and Lisaweta lies precisely in this adolescent-like tonality: 'It's all just metaphysics, music and eroticism for adolescents'.[7] This is an adolescent-like quality reached late, finally, by authors just under thirty (Lukács was twenty-six or twenty-seven when he wrote 'On Poverty of Spirit'— more or less the same age as Mann at the time of *Tonio Kröger*): a precarious state, threatened both by childhood and by maturity, though one would wish to abide there. It is precarious and subject to the threats of before and after until it is grounded and stabilized indefinitely by a death—it sounds too rhetorical to say 'by a human sacrifice', but that is the sense,—whether the death of a youth, Hanno Buddenbrook; of an adult, Thomas Buddenbrook; or even of somebody in one's age group: Lukács wrote 'On Poverty of Spirit' after the suicide of Irma Seidler. It might be the death of a character, or of a

---

6 Thomas Mann, *Epistolario 1889–1936* (E. Mann ed., I. A. Chiusano trans.) (Milan: Mondadori, 1963) / *The Letters of Heinrich and Thomas Mann, 1900–1949* (Hans Wysling ed., Don Reneau trans.) (Berkeley CA: University of California Press, 1998) [translation modified].

7 Mann, *Epistolario*.

real person. It might be the death of one who, like the child or the adult, jeopardizes the adolescent-like tonality by setting time limits on it; or the death of someone who shares in that tonality (or perhaps even only in the hard work needed to achieve it), and by dying makes that tonality as permanent as his image, now unchangeable, is for the survivor. Just leafing through any one of the German manuals of scholastic ethics of those times is enough to find definitions of suicide as the sign of the 'incapability or unwillingness' to 'accomplish a task'; and it is perhaps not casual that, in those manuals, the pages on suicide are immediately followed by those on the 'Duties of Goodness' (the various categories of 'duty' usually determining the arrangement of the subject matter)[8]. In Lukács's dialogue, while the male character, for all his interest in the frescoes of the cemetery of Pisa, ends up as the *impuissant Orcagna* in a variant of Baudelaire's sonnet 'Le mauvais moine' (though its standard version reads: *O moine fainéant!*)[9], the suicide woman reverses this ethics and, in light of others failing to perform the 'duties of goodness', posits her own suicide as a forced 'ability and willingness' to 'accomplish a task'.

It was to Irma Seidler that Lukács dedicated *Soul and Form*, the work in which his adolescent-like tonality became an enduring situation. To give a foundation to that adolescent-like tonality, a death was needed. The

---

8 August Döring, *Handbuch der menschlich-natürlichen Sittenlehre für Eltern und Erzieher* (Stuttgart: Frommann, 1899), pp.139–40.

9 Charles Baudelaire, *Œuvres* (Y.G. LeDantec annot.) (Paris: Gallimard, 1956), p. 1386 / *The Complete Verse* (Francis Scarfe trans.) (Manchester: Carcanet Press, 2012). The standard version of the original sonnet reads: 'O moine fainéant! [*Impuissant Orcagna!*] quand saurai-je donc faire / Du spectacle vivant de ma triste misère / Le travail de mes mains et l'amour de mes yeux?'

aesthetics of that adolescent-like tonality—an ontological aesthetics, measuring the limits of existence and life experience—had as its foundational axiom ('metaphysics, music and eroticism for adolescents') the dying *in* someone, being destroyed in someone, so that the cry would reach a vibration of such height as to result in silence. The contrast in both Thomas Mann and Lukács vis-à-vis the aesthetics and metaphysics of Expressionism lies first and foremost in this: both were unwilling to abide in the adolescent-like tonality of that self-destruction in someone. Unlike the Expressionists, they were unwilling to indefinitely prefer death and the tension of the cry towards silence, and consequently to configure present time as the time of a final battle, of a last night in which even the possibilities of an erotic, individual or political and social victory were to warrant necessary defeat because of the need for an antinomian, radical, utopian renewal of anything that was structure and super-structure, form, reality whether existing or imaginable.

With Expressionism, the late adolescent-like tonality achieved by intellectuals and artists in the first years of the century was subjected to a concentration on itself, an exploitation of its own limits that became programmatic, an enjoyment of this tonality as such, that turned it from an indefinitely safe haven into the 'heaven' and 'hell'[10] of

---

10 'Men will always live in their own age as I do. But why has it struck me, of all people? The blameless are struck. One is struck, the other is struck. One is spared, the other is spared. What do we know? Where? How? Each dawn can bring paradise; each night, hell'—see Ernst Toller, 'Lo sciancato' in Vito Pandolfi (ed.), *Teatro espressionista tedesco* (Parma: Guanda, 1956). We have modified the translation to read 'in their own *age*' rather than 'in their own time'. [See 'Hinkemann' (Vera Mendel trans.) in *Seven Plays* (London: John Lane, 1935)—Trans.].

the late adolescent, the inescapable point of departure for the 'East Pole'[11]. Lukács's progress to Marxism, on the other hand, signals his forsaking of that adolescence, just like, for Thomas Mann, that forsaking lies in the gradual progress from the stories of the Buddenbrooks and Tonio Kröger to that of an 'ordinary', 'simple' (*einfach*) person like Hans Castorp, and finally in the chance, seized with lightning-quick dexterity, of becoming (as himself, as Mann) an emblem of antifascism. Lukács's liking for Mann, or at least his effort to save Mann's work within a Marxist perspective, in fact *also* seems to be the confirmation of an affinity, of a fundamental ethical choice common to both: the refusal of the adolescent-like tonality that both had achieved well past adolescence, and the refusal (recognized more or less arbitrarily as a further common denominator) of what had brought both to the late achievement of that tonality: the original sin of bourgeois culture, 'metaphysics, music and eroticism for adolescents', the blockade of intellectuals in that haven, the shorts that actors—like adolescents grown too fast—wore in the early productions of *Spring Awakening* at the Deutsches Theater,[12] the bourgeois ban on intellectuals and artists wearing trousers even at seventy (the only alternative being the trousers of a military uniform, since the academic outfit, the evening jacket or suit, the tails and the bohemian attire all are shorts, no matter if metaphorical). The power of this ban, which bourgeois culture is able to enforce on its wayward, fugitive or

---

11 *Ostpolzug* [Journey to the East Pole], a play by Arnolt Bronnen, which premiered at the Berlin Prussian State Theatre in January 1926.

12 See Furio Jesi, 'Thomas Mann', *Il Castoro* 67–68 (November 1972): 4–5.

apostate artists and intellectuals even from a great distance, can be gauged by considering how both Mann and Lukács, having sought to elude it (in two ways that are different but close, because both consist of adopting a political habit), in fact failed to escape the lifelong condition of minority that was prescribed for them. This can sound like a very harsh, or simply rash, hasty and superficial judgement—even more so, perhaps, towards Lukács than towards Mann, if only because the political quality of Lukács's work after he moved on to Marxism is doubtlessly much less second-hand than that of Mann's output as a *praeceptor* of antifascism. But even in Lukács's case the passage from a work like *History and Class Consciousness* to his subsequent production seems to us much more similar to a backwards itinerary from the culmination of adolescence to a childhood miming maturity and searching for its models in classical culture rather than in the risks of adolescence. Is this actual maturity? We might want to ask whether bourgeois culture, sometimes accused of having directly produced or (by being a vacuum to be filled) indirectly caused the myth of happy childhood, might not in fact have created another even more deceptive myth to which the childhood myth is merely a corollary: that is, the myth of maturity. A particularly deceptive myth, not because it promises a happy age that is in fact devoid of any happiness—there is happiness in power—but because it promises an *age*, to which in fact only *years* correspond: some *years* (of possible power) rather than an *age*, a tonality of discourse, a state of mind, affects and also habitual behaviours, that are in fact configured as a real complex only for the real *ages*: adolescence and old age. Real, that is, within the only framework that we have directly under our eyes, that of bourgeois society, in which childhood and maturity are not *ages* but duration— duration *undergone* without being able to conquer and use it as a place of stability, to transform it into one's own skin, precisely because one is in some measure powerful in a more than symbolic way. A purely symbolic power is enjoyed by the old (meaning the really old, that is the forsaken and the solitary, rather than those who retain real power through many years, therefore continuing to have years instead of age), and by adolescents, 'in reserve for the future'; both the old and the adolescent require caution, but do not otherwise impinge on the actual exercise of power. But one who abides in childhood does have power, for not only does she require cautions, but, owing to her intrinsic weakness (similar to that of the old) and—crucially—to the importance of her survival (dissimilar to that of the old), she has a right to the decidedly unsymbolic power of having subordinates. As scarcely symbolic, tautologically unsymbolic, is the power of the 'mature man', i.e. the man who is par excellence endowed with power. And those whose power is not only symbolic do not have *age*, but rather *years*. Within bourgeois society the exercise of power, albeit in the more elementary forms of the power of childhood, is what prevents one from overcoming time, from making it one's home: for those who have power, years are counted, just like they are counted—backwards—in prison; one is sentenced to five, fifteen, twenty years of power, and the counting is done either by those who rec- ognize that power (when those who possess it cannot exercise it in full awareness—as is the case with children, who, however, soon learn to count the years) or by those who possess it and consciously exercise it (the 'mature' man). But neither the years of adolescence nor those of old age are counted—for they *cannot* be counted. Both adolescence and old age are victories over time, imposing onto time tonalities of discourse, states of mind, affects and habitual behaviours that find within themselves their own atemporal norm. This does not in any way mean that to be of an *age* instead of having some *years*, to be an adolescent or an old man instead of being a child or a 'mature' man is more pleasant or gives one an easier life. We might say that the opposite is almost obviously true. Neither does it mean that this shall always be the case, given the traits characterizing the human species. Our entire discourse is directly and exclusively referred to the relationships between man, time and power within bourgeois society; neither can it be objected that in today's world millions of children are in fact deprived of even the power to live, while millions of old people only 'overcome' time by turning it into a skin of rigidly habitual behaviours that move us more to horror than to pity. The relationships between man, time and power that we have shown are exclusively those referred to the *model* of existence resulting from the consistent prolongation of the lines in the geometry of bourgeois society—lines that society is concerned with presenting as mere segments. 'When form is shattered against the rocks of existence', concrete power in fact also becomes symbolic, while symbolic power seems to take on a ghostly sort of concreteness. Only death, which is not contemplated in Lukács's essay on Kierkegaard but appears twice and is almost concentrated on itself—as suicide—in 'On Poverty of Spirit', intervenes to eliminate confusion and clarify the relationships between man, time and power in the exemplification of bourgeois society—as well as clarifying who, according to that model, really has only some years (and power), and who really has only 'age' (and no power). Only death, when it appears, can truly bring to light the model of bourgeois society and culture, in the course of a reaction configured, as it may be, within the scope of aesthetics, of religion, or that admixture of aesthetics and religion that is the *religio mortis*. In the essay on Kierkegaard we find a forsaking, not a death. But we are left wondering whether the version of Irma Seidler's suicide given by Lukács might not be an equivalent of the relationship of forsaking between Kierkegaard and Regine Olsen. Real-life forsaking, real-life suicide: both taking place in history. In 'On Poverty of Spirit' we find two suicides: the woman, and later the man who was unable to prevent her suicide because he was devoid of 'poverty of spirit', of the ability to cause form to shatter against the ahistorical 'I' (victorious over time) of the late adolescent, rather than 'against the rocks of existence'. The relationship of forsaking—to use once again this paradoxical expression, which is however no paradox within the adolescent-like condition of destroying oneself in somebody, to the extent of forsaking that somebody through having taken one's self from him by destroying it in him—is in our view the norm of the twofold suicide, not because each of the suicides was destroyed in the other, but because this model of mutual self-destruction is the norm, *unactualized* in reality, that holds all the real, adolescent-like tonalities of discourse, states of mind, affects and perspectives of habitual behaviour in literary unreality. There is a chamber, a space victorious over time and hence adolescent-like, in which they both found themselves, blindly feeling towards each other for the direction of their own self-destruction in *an* other. The suicide woman left that chamber first, alone, and was then followed. She did in fact leave, but her death became the human sacrifice—here the expression can be used without sounding rhetorical—thanks to which bourgeois culture offers the survivor, the merely nominal suicide, an apparent way out. Which is only Orpheus' way out of the chamber of the living / the adolescents, into the dark corridor leading to a Eurydice who has become a part of the realm of the dead, the powerful, of those who, whether children or 'mature' men, have *years*, not *age*. As is well known, Orpheus *must* turn around, *must* return to that adolescent-like chamber, which is the space reserved by bourgeois culture to the practice of poetry. Bourgeois culture does not contemplate or allow for the full effectiveness of *a* death, much less so of a death *in* somebody. The *religio mortis* that sometimes comes to its surface is a religion *of death*, not of *a* death. *A* death may mean dying *in* somebody; *death* means the dying of each person alone, just like each person *possesses* alone, having power, having years—but not age. Bachofen said that the space of the tomb is the generating nucleus of private property: and indeed it is, but of course only because the tomb is the tomb of *one*, one who exits the chamber alone or remains there alone. The same cannot be said of the shared tombs of Tristan and Isolde or Romeo and Juliet, which besides, precisely because our horror of property has infected us with horror and a sense of dutiful contempt for corpses and tombs (similar to the Manichees' abhorrence of any linguistic expressions referring to 'eating'), we don't see as tombs, because they are not the tomb *of one*. If anything, they are the depths of the sea: '*A grant espleit s'en vont par l'onde, / trenchant s'en vont la mer parfonde*'.[13]

The two Christian religious emblems opening and closing Lukács's piece (the fresco of Judgement Day in the cemetery of Pisa and the words from the Apocalypse) might be seen as the eschatological framework for the adolescent-like age of the double tomb. But in this case they take on a double function: on one hand they point to the closed form of a twofold dying in somebody, represented by the two suicides and symbolizing the, so to speak, positive quality of the adolescent-like age; on the other hand, they point to the guilt incurred by the merely literary suicide (while Seidler actually died, Lukács only had his male character die, not himself) and the fracture through which ethics penetrates the adolescent-like age—'Goodness is not an ethical category. You'll find it in no consistent ethical system'. If the characters of the two suicides in Lukács's piece were not relating to a different external reality, or if we wished to see that piece as a self-sufficient, enclosed sphere, the second suicide would close the harmony hinted at by the first, there would be two joined tombs, and the two Christian eschatological

---

13 See Gaston Paris, *Poèmes et légendes du Moyen Age* (Paris: Société d'Édition Artistique, 1900), p. 123.

symbols would have the function of keeping ethics visibly away from that harmony and that age. Even the Last Judgement can become the symbol of an estrangement of ethics or of its suspension, if the Last Judgement is recognized as the pausing par excellence of *years* and a justification of *ages*—no matter whether such justification is a condemnation or an approval: heaven and hell both belong to *age*, not *years*; *ages* are outside ethics, which, passing judgement on *years*, intervenes as soon as power does. 'The living life is beyond forms, ordinary life is on this side of them': to live through *years* means living through 'ordinary life', i.e. serving years in the prison 'on this side of forms'. To live through *ages* means living within time and within enclosed modalities—enclosed because they must prelude to the advent of 'goodness' that breaks forms ('and goodness is the grace to shatter these forms'). Time and the enclosed modalities of the adolescent age or of old age are neither 'the living life' nor 'ordinary life'; they are at the same time 'beyond' and 'on this side of' forms; they are thus in that situation outside ethics and power that alone allows us to expect to be able 'to shatter forms'. *Age* is always the preamble to an eschatological subversion which would be 'If you like: the true life, the living life'. But we must stress that 'If you like', which here is not some banal rhetorical clause, but rather truly implies a certain suspiciousness as to the exactness of the definition that follows. We may well call that eschatological subversion 'real life, the living life'; but strictly speaking, the expression 'the living life' is only appropriate to the instant in which it is contrasted to 'ordinary life', since forms remain as an intact barrier between one and the other 'life'. When goodness intervenes to shatter forms, 'the living life' no longer is an exact definition for what was 'beyond forms'; the eschatological subversion cannot give results that are in any way predictable, not even predictable by an apparently generic definition: 'Life, however, can neither be nor become pure'.

But even 'ordinary life' no longer is an exact definition for what was 'this side of forms', if goodness intervenes to shatter forms. And this is, in our view, where the most delirious core of 'On Poverty of Spirit' is found: its more evident mystical schema, in which Lukács tends to identify the male character with the Christ, and the two women—the suicide and her sister, who is in dialogue with the 'Christ'—with Mary and Martha. Through the tangle of Mitteleuropean culture by which this schema is articulated (Meister Eckhart, but also the *Frivolität* that immediately leads us to think, with hindsight, of the dandy in Baudelaire/Benjamin), we can make out a more enigmatic contraposition than that between 'practical ethics and worldly activity', given the enigmatic character of the third term joined to the two, i.e. the sacrifice of a suicide Christ. It is extremely difficult today to formulate any hypothesis as to the weight of Lukács's Jewish origins relative to his choice of creating a counterfigure for himself (the male character in 'On Poverty of Spirit') that was a sort of suicide Christ. The entire connotation of the characters in that piece along Christian mystical lines has, we repeat, a shifting, delirious quality that is not allayed by the cultural commonplaces, recurring though they may be on every page (it would be easy, for example, to read 'On Poverty of Spirit' in a Rilkean key—all the more so since the cultural atmosphere was the same: and in the same issue of the *Neue Blätter*[14] where it was published for the first and last time, Lukács's piece immediately precedes Rilke's *Aus dem Marien-Leben* [pp. 93ff.]; not to speak of the Rilkean themes of 'poverty', St Francis,[15] etc.). Doubtlessly, this irruption of *delira-menta* (*apocryphorum?*) into the extremely neat philo-sophical construction that would be fine-tuned once and for all in *Soul and Form* leaves us with the suspicion that, faced with Seidler's suicide, Lukács 'the Jew' might have conflated the bad conscience of his surviving the suicide woman with the bad conscience of the false Christian handling Christian symbols as his own, finding a confirmation of the falseness of the male character (a suicide for love, 'like Christ', but unlike Lukács) in the falseness of an apologetics paving the way for what was left of 'ordinary life' after goodness had shattered the 'forms'. The non-correspondence between literary work and life, the fact that there were two suicides in the literary work but only one in life, could be seen as the breach through the *age* of adolescence that gave Lukács a way out in his search for *years*. The death of Irma

---

14 Reference to *Neue Blatter* 5–6 (1912). [Trans.]

15 'But the other alternative—there's surely no death about that. No death in Jesus or St Francis, for example.'

'In spots,' said Rampion. 'They were dead in spots. Very much alive in others, I quite agree. But they simply left half of existence out of account. No, no, they won't do. It's time people stopped talking about them. I'm tired of Jesus and Francis, terribly tired of them.' See Aldous Huxley, *Point Counter Point* (David Bradshaw introd.) (London: Vintage, 2004), p. 156. In the original, Jesi quotes from the Italian translation: *Punto contro punto* (S. Spaventa Filippi trans.) (Milan: Sonzogno, 1933). [Trans.]

Seidler, like the eschatological Christian emblems opening and closing 'On Poverty of Spirit', would then truly acquire a precise twofold significance: perfecting of the age of adolescence and first moment of the eschatological subversion; but also, at the same time, exit from the age of adolescence, and entry into the years of having power, and of being therefore liable to judgement.

# An Analysis of the Mythological Language in the Book of Daniel, 13

EDITOR'S NOTE

The following text is the most important among Jesi's unpublished papers and is, for several reasons, absolutely central to his production. Written around 1970, it stems from the strand of research that began with 'Le connessioni archetipiche'[1] and found one of its highest points in his 1962 essay, 'Il tentato adulterio mitico in Grecia e in Egitto'.[2]

In this essay, Jesi illustrates, perhaps better than anywhere else, his conception of 'mythological language' as a system endowed with internal autonomy and organized along a set of recognizable relationships stabilized by the predominance of a few 'privileged' elements. By studying the biblical text and its connections with Genesis 37–50, as well as its analogies with Hellenistic literature, Elamite or Ugaritic mythology and onomastics (the *Legend of Dan-El*) or with the mythology of conversion in the apocryphal Joseph and Aseneth, Jesi sheds light on a consistent development of figures (Rachel, Bilhah, Susanna) and regulating norms. He explores a space in mythological language that is at the same time a place of indeterminacy relative to licit vs illicit and a place 'of coincidence between Babylon and the Jews'.

Now, if the 'privilege' of the 'Bateau ivre' rested in its paradigmatic status (a work made out of the matter of 'commonplaces' that in turn becomes a commonplace or a 'thing');

---

1 Furio Jesi, 'Le connessioni archetipiche', *Archivio internazionale di etnografia e preistoria* 1 (1958): 35– 44. [Trans.]

2 Furio Jesi, 'Il tentato adulterio mitico in Grecia e in Egitto', *Aegyptus* 42(3–4) (July–December 1962): 276–96. [Trans.]

if in Rilke the 'interrelations' between Sonnets and Elegies governed the separation between the content and the asemantic core of the commonplaces, the privilege of the mythology of Susanna rests in the confluence of foreign mythological and ritual elements, which however, for the exiled, bilingual Jew of Hellenism resonate as absolutely profane (the bath spied upon by the Elders is profane) and 'float'—in Jesi's words— as naked forms susceptible to taking on any form. We might perhaps add that this privilege is, for the exiled mythologist, the ultimate floating of science in the naked form of self-portrait—or, by the closest connection of scholarship and life, the emerging of a self-portrait in mythological form.

Although consisting of a complete text, with a few handwritten amendments showing the author's revisions, the typescript was left without notes. As well as the reference (in connection with Tiresias and Oedipus) to the second volume of Kerényi's *Mythologie der Griechen* (1958) and to great studies mentioned more or less directly, such as the 1965 classic *Hellenosemitica* by Michael C. Astour (whose critique of Victor Bérard Jesi shared, and whose work on the Sumerian deity Shuzianna he drew upon) or Martin Braun's *History and Romance in Graeco-Oriental Literature* (1938), we can easily recognize his debt towards Jozef Vergote's groundbreaking study, *Joseph en Égypte* (1959), of which Jesi rereads especially the paragraphs on 'Le commerce des gommes et des résines' (on labdanum, gum tragacanth, balm) and 'La femme infidèle' (on the story of Joseph and Potiphar's wife).

## An Analysis of the Mythological Language
## in the Book of Daniel, 13

### 1. 'FOR IT WAS HOT WEATHER'

If considered as an evocation of the epiphany of a nude
female figure at her bath viewed by those who, unseen, can
see her and wish to be sexually joined with her, the text of
Daniel 13 finds within earlier and roughly contemporaneous Jewish[1] literary tradition at least two homologues:
II Samuel 11:2ff., Bathsheba and David; the Testaments of
the Twelve Patriarchs, Testament of Reuben, Bilhah and
Reuben. The text of II Samuel is certainly earlier than the
one in Daniel 13, whereas the Testament of Reuben does
not seem to date back any earlier than the second century
BCE and can thus be configured, from a chronological point
of view, within the cultural environment in which Daniel
13 was written.

The homology between these three texts, deduced
from the fact that each of them shows the motif, or rather
the cluster of motifs, we have mentioned (epiphany of a
nude female figure at her bath, etc.), can be used as a
working hypothesis for a not too superficial analysis of
the mythological language in Daniel 13 only if, within

---

1 The Italian 'ebraico' (n. & adj.) carries the multiple meanings of
'Jewish', 'Hebraic' and 'Hebrew language'. For consistency, I have used
'Jewish' or 'Hebrew [language]' throughout. [Trans.]

that cluster of motifs, we can pinpoint one or more mythological elements that are at the same time 'perspicuous' in
the cultural context of the three texts and, within the
restricted purview, the enclosed system of each of them,
can be thought of—by ourselves, today—as privileged
elements, conditioning factors par excellence of the mutual
relationships between all of the several components of
each system. An analysis of the *mythological* language of
a text in fact consists of choosing as a subject, among
the many languages recognizable within a linguistic
document, one language—declared as *mythological*—
such as can be thought of as a context of totalizing
elements, all functioning in such a way as to condition,
according to an absolutely self-justifying norm, the
other, non-privileged linguistic elements.

The word 'elements' should not necessarily call to
mind any figures, images, personae or objects liable to be
at least theoretically isolated as autonomous figurations.
'Elements' can be—and often, in this sense, are—
connections, relationships. In the case of the three texts
we shall examine here, the first element that seems at the
same time perspicuous within their general cultural
context and privileged within the enclosed system of each
is precisely one relationship: that between a female figure
at her bath and the sexual union.

Bathsheba is seen nude at her bath by David, who later
sends for the woman and joins with her. Bilhah is seen nude
at her bath by Reuben; a while later, Reuben happens upon
Bilhah sleeping nude and drunken in her chamber, and
joins with her. Susanna is seen nude at her bath by the
Elders, who immediately afterwards proposition her and
are met with her refusal. In our view, the document

which, in particular, opens a chink on the importance of the relationship between a female figure at her bath and sexual union is the Testament of Reuben. Reuben sees Bilhah nude twice: first while she is bathing 'in a covered place', and later in her chamber. Only after the second time does Reuben join with Bilhah, but he states that without the first time—without having seen Bilhah nude at her bath—he would not have sinned (the nature of that sin is later defined with a technical term, πορνεία, in Reuben 1:6):

> For had I not seen Bilhah bathing in a covered place, I had not fallen into this great iniquity. For my mind taking in the thought of the woman's nakedness, suffered me not to sleep until I had wrought the abominable thing.
> (Reuben 3:11–12)

These words build within the Testament of Reuben a sequence of interconnected elements, whose consistency can be recognized in the fact that three of them become especially significant because set in a state of mutual tension. A first element is Bilhah's blamelessness. Bilhah is not guilty, because Reuben joins with her only the second time, taking advantage of her when he finds her in a drunken sleep: 'Having therefore gone in and beheld her nakedness, I wrought the impiety, and leaving her sleeping I departed' (Reuben 3:14). Things would be different if Reuben had joined with Bilhah the first time he saw her, nude and not asleep, at her bath. Otherwise, to save Bilhah's blamelessness, the story should contain an element that is in fact absent: violence brutal enough to prevent self-defence, perpetrated by Reuben on a wide-awake Bilhah. The absence of this element is connected with the presence of another, that takes on special significance in the text: the fact that Reuben's guilt is due not to his being always and anyway a sinner, but to his young age (ἐν ἀγνοίᾳ νεότητος), his momentary weakness, his powerlessness to resist a twice-repeated temptation that, in correspondence with Bilhah's blamelessness, appears on both occasions as the work of one of the seven 'tempting spirits'—the spirit of fornication. In post-biblical Jewish exegesis, the epiphany of Bathsheba nude at her bath before David's eyes was in fact the work of the will of YHWH, who had decided to test David (Sanhedrin 107a). The Testament of Reuben, however, stresses that the decisive moment of temptation was the bath, so that the relationship between a female figure at her bath and sexual union is presented as the third, interconnected element of special significance.

The words of II Samuel 11 would lead us to deduce a connection between the bath of Bathsheba when David saw her and the *mikveh*, the ritual bath taken by Jewish women after menstruation. II Samuel (11:4) tells us that, when David sent for Bathsheba after seeing her nude at her bath: 'she came in unto him; and he lay with her, for she was purified from her monthly uncleanness.' The fact that the bath during which Bathsheba was seen by David is connected with the ritual bath also seems to find confirmation in another version (Sanhedrin 107a): Satan appeared to David in the form of a bird; David shot an arrow that missed the bird and broke a wicker screen behind which Bathsheba was combing her hair; thus the king saw her and desired her. One of what we know as 'Ezra's Rules' (Baba Kamma 82a–82b; Ketubot 5a; Baba Batra 22a) prescribes that the hair be combed for the ritual bath.

In the Jewish tradition the ritual bath, and particularly the bath after menstruation, is an indispensable preliminary condition to a woman having sexual intercourse. In II Targum Esther (4:13–14), Mordecai mentions as especially evil the behaviour of Sisera, who banned the Jews from accessing water springs and thus prevented their women performing the ritual baths and hence having sexual intercourse: in the Jewish tradition, the ritual bath necessarily precedes ritually legitimate sexual unions. In II Samuel 11, the bath, connected with the ritual bath and becoming the occasion on which a man, unseen, sees the nude woman, precedes an illicit sexual union (illicit not for reasons of impurity, but because it infringes the ban on adultery). In the Testament of Reuben, the bath, which in the text as such seems unconnected with the ritual bath and becomes the occasion on which a man, unseen, sees the nude woman, precedes an illicit sexual union (also illicit not for reasons of impurity, but because it infringes the ban on adultery, with the aggravating circumstance that this time the adultery is committed by a man with his father's wife). The Testament of Reuben is certainly later than the text of II Samuel, and was written in the context of a culture in which II Samuel was not only perfectly well known, but considered a sacred text. In both cases, the reasons for the woman's bath should be seen in light of the relationship of semantic compensation that, from this point of view, connects the two texts: in the earlier text (II Sam 11), Bathsheba's bath is connected to the ritual bath; in the more recent one (Reuben), Bilhah's bath is apparently unconnected with the ritual bath, but this is compensated by its being declared as the prime reason for the fornication, with the open admission that simply seeing the nude woman—the second time—would not of itself have caused the sin. In both cases, the ultimate reason for the woman's bath as an occasion of temptation is ascribed to the will of YHWH or to the intervention of one of the 'seven tempting spirits', and this holds true for the Rabbinical exegesis of both texts, configuring them both within the general context of Jewish culture (relatively static in this respect). However, an analysis of each of the texts as enclosed systems *as well as* documents of a wider system (i.e., as we have seen, the general context of Jewish culture) shows that the immediate reason for Bathsheba's bath is connected to that of the ritual, as is the immediate—albeit undeclared through the literal elements of the text—reason for Bilhah's bath. The ritual bath, when not sullied by a man who, unseen, sees the nude woman, necessarily precedes ritually legitimate sexual unions. Within the scope of non-mythological language, the unsullied ritual bath need not necessarily precede (ritually legitimate) sexual unions. But within the scope of mythological language, the sullied ritual bath is presented as necessarily preceding illicit (because adulterous) sexual unions. If, within the scope of non-mythological language, the woman, after the unsullied ritual bath, *need not* necessarily join with a man, within the scope of mythological language the woman, after the sullied ritual bath, must necessarily join with a man in an illicit union. This holds within the context of both II Samuel 11 and the Testament of Reuben.

In Daniel 13, however, Susanna's bath is explicitly defined as *non-ritual*: Susanna thought she would 'wash herself in the orchard; for it was hot weather' (Dan, 13:15), and the fact that she was spied while bathing implies not the *necessity* but the *proposition* of an illicit sexual union. Thus the three texts under consideration are ruled by the following norm: if the bath during which the woman is spied is connected with the ritual bath (whether directly as in II Samuel 11 or indirectly, through stressing the bath, rather than the simple seeing of the nude woman, as the motive of fornication, as in the Testament of Reuben), then the presence of men spying the nude woman is a profanation not only of her nudity, but also of the ritual action in which her nudity is involved, and thus corresponds to the necessity of the illicit sexual union that follows. If, on the other hand, the bath during which the woman is spied is unconnected with the ritual bath ('for it was hot weather'—Dan, 13:15), the presence of men spying the nude woman is only a profanation of her nudity, independent of any ritual action in which her nudity may be involved, and thus corresponds not to the *necessity* but only to the *proposition* of an illicit sexual union, that the woman will refuse.

## 2. Susanna as a Third Rachel

In the phase of the analysis of Daniel 13 in which the proposition of an illicit sexual union and its refusal become salient within the relationship between a female figure at her bath and sexual union, the story of Susanna and the Elders seems to show some affinity with the story of Joseph and Potiphar's wife in Genesis (39:7ff). Like Joseph, Susanna refuses the illicit proposition and is or is about to be, albeit partially, subjected to the penal consequences of the slander by which those who propositioned her take revenge for her refusal. The 'motif' we might label as 'Joseph and Potiphar's wife' is found in a huge number of versions in worldwide literature, and the mere fact of its presence—in a version much differentiated from the others—in Daniel 13 could not lead to any plausible hypothesis. One first sign of a special relationship between the story of Susanna and the story of Joseph consists of the particular interest aroused by Genesis (39:7ff) within Jewish culture roughly contemporaneous to the writing of Daniel 13: suffice it to think of the Testament of Joseph and the elaborations of the story in Philo and in Flavius Josephus. M. Braun cited hardly refutable arguments in support of the theory that the writing of the Testament of Joseph (and later Flavius Josephus, Ant. 2:39–59) bears substantial traces of the version of the story of Hippolytus and Phaedra in Euripides' *Hyppolytos*. This reference to Euripides might be the first step towards a reading of the story of Joseph and Potiphar's wife in which its post-biblical elaborations may be connected both to Daniel 13 and to Joseph and Aseneth (and hence to the pseudo-epigraph that might provide an answer to the question: '*Le judaïsme de la Diaspora, et tout particulièrement le judaïsme de la Diaspora égyptienne, a-t-il permis que se développe en son sein un culte marqué par l'influence des cultes à mystères?*').[2]

A starting point is the fact that during Hellenism some Jewish authors used for their elaboration of the story of Joseph a document like Euripides' *Hyppolytos*, in which the 'motif' of the woman who offers herself to a man and, finding herself rejected, accuses him of attempted rape shows a very clear slant towards the 'motif' of incest. In Euripides the figure of Phaedra as mother-bride to Hippolytus comes to the surface with particular clarity. In Genesis (39:7ff), nothing seems to

---

2 'Has diaspora Judaism, and in particular Egyptian diaspora Judaism, allowed the development at its core of a cult influenced by sacred mysteries?' [Trans.]

show Potiphar's wife as in any way having a motherly function towards Joseph. In the post-biblical tradition, however, we find the statement that the girl Aseneth, future wife to Joseph, was the daughter of Potiphar and his wife (and the problem posed by the existence of a daughter of Potiphar the *eunuch* has been considered and variously solved by Philo and by the Haggadah). Thus Joseph refuses the illicit union with Potiphar's wife and later celebrates his wedding with her daughter. Traditionally, Potiphar's wife is Joseph's future mother-in-law, and is thus related to Joseph by a sort of 'precarious' motherhood, like Phaedra (the step-mother) was related to Hippolytus.

'Precarious' motherhood does not mean true and proper motherhood. But in the case of Phaedra and Hippolytus, the precariousness of the motherly condition is precisely correlated with the transformation of the ban on incest into the refusal of a sexual union on the part of the 'son'. To what extent is this situation homologous with Hellenistic elaborations of the story of Joseph?

Joseph's mother is Rachel. Rachel dies after giving birth to Benjamin when Joseph is still a small child. Joseph has a second mother: Bilhah. All the texts in the post-biblical tradition make of Bilhah a second Rachel. Bilhah is born on the same day as Rachel. After Rachel's (and Leah's?) death, Jacob legitimizes Bilhah and Zilpah as his wives. The moon in Joseph's dream alludes to Bilhah, his second mother, and not to Rachel. It is Bilhah who always mediates between Joseph and his father: Bilhah who tells Joseph that Jacob is sick; Bilhah who conveys the message from dying Jacob to Joseph on behalf of his brothers. Bilhah's son, Naphtali, conceived after Rachel has given Bilhah to Jacob, is born on Rachel's knees and is physically identical to Joseph. Before dying, Joseph names Rachel's tomb on the way to Ephrath (the tomb of the mother par excellence) as the tomb of Rachel and Bilhah.

Rachel is the privileged favourite among Jacob's wives—and among the mothers of the Jewish people: 'A cry was heard in Ramah' (Gen 31:15); and she is blameless, the victim of a ruse (through which her father first offers Leah to Jacob, who is unaware of the swap). Bilhah, as a second Rachel, is also privileged but is guilty, or at least connected with guilt, through her illicit union with Reuben. Bilhah's connection with guilt derives from the bath during which she was seen by Reuben. The ruse of which Rachel—the privileged wife, the blameless one—was a victim took the form of a sexual union in which the man (Jacob) could not see the woman (Leah in lieu of Rachel) in the dark. The first Rachel, the blameless one, becomes a victim because of a sexual union consummated 'out of sight' to her detriment.

The second Rachel (Bilhah) is connected with guilt because of a sexual union consummated to her detriment because a man (Reuben) saw her while remaining unseen. The first Rachel is subjected to an 'absence of sight' consisting of the fact that the man (Jacob) cannot see the woman with whom he is joining (Leah). The second Rachel is subjected to an 'absence of sight' consisting of the fact that she cannot see the man who spies her nudity. We might wonder whether Susanna might not be the third Rachel, who like the first and second is subjected to an 'absence of sight': like the second Rachel, she does not see that she is being seen nude, and like the first, does not acquire through this 'absence of sight' a connection with guilt, since she will refuse sexual union with those who saw her.

The point of coincidence between the second and the third Rachel (between Bilhah and Susanna) lies in the connection between the epiphany of the nude woman at her bath and the sexual union. Since the moment of her connection with the image of the spied-upon bath, Rachel gives rise to a second and a third Rachel: the former connected with guilt (because her bath is connected with the ritual), the latter blameless (because her bath is not connected with the ritual bath). The bath is the occasion for the displaying of nudity. Rachel is not only Jacob's privileged wife, but the privileged mother of the Jewish people. Rachel's bath is the occasion for the displaying of the mother's nudity: when the bath is 'ritual', as in the case of the second Rachel, the mother's nudity is spied by the 'son' (Reuben) and the 'absence of sight' implicit in the being spied translates into an illicit sexual union (incestuous as well as adulterous) with the spying man; when the bath is not ritual, as in the case of the third Rachel (Susanna), the mother's nudity is spied by those (the Elders) who *cannot* be her sons, and the 'absence of sight' implicit in the being spied upon translates only into the refused proposition of an illicit sexual union.

All this serves to outline the ritual character of the bath in the texts of the Testament of Reuben and Daniel 13. The bath is ritual, during which the mother's nudity is spied by the son as a prelude to incest. The bath is non-ritual, during which the mother's nudity is spied by those who cannot be her sons as a prelude to the proposition of an illicit union that will be refused. The 'absence of sight' is the space of mythological language within which the sexual union can take place as an illicit (Bilhah and Reuben) or licit (Susanna and the Elders) relationship with the mother's nudity. The relationship between Susanna and the Elders is in fact a 'licit' version of the relationship with the mother's nudity, in that the mother is spied by those who, whilst being her sons (as every Jew is the son of Rachel), cannot be her sons (the Elders), and their condition is confirmed by the refusal on the part of the mother (Susanna). The 'absence of sight' taking place in the case of the wedding between Jacob and Leah (in lieu of Rachel) is the space open to licit vs illicit, and the ambiguity between Leah and Rachel within that space (the bride is 'Rachel', but is Leah) corresponds to the availability of that space, embracing both the licit and the illicit—just like, in the extra-Jewish cultural context in which the Testament of Reuben and Daniel 13 are situated, the epiphany of the nude female figure at her bath is the sight at the same time most worth seeing and most forbidden.

In the *Lauacrum Palladis*, Callimachus tells us that Athena was seen nude while bathing in the Hippocrene by young Tiresias, and as a punishment made him blind. In the following pages, he adds that Artemis had Actaeon devoured by his own hounds because he had seen the goddess nude at her bath. In earlier documents, Actaeon's punishment was given a different reason: Euripides (*Bacchae*) states that Artemis had Actaeon devoured by the hounds because he had boasted that he could better her in the art of hunting. We shall examine these documents in detail later. For the moment, we are interested in noting preliminarily that the motif of the goddess seen nude at her bath is certainly documented in Hellenistic culture before the writing of the Testament of Reuben and Daniel 13 (a story analogous to that evoked in the

*Lauacrum Palladis* is also found in Antoninus Liberalis 17.5: Artemis was seen nude at her bath by the Cretan Siproites, and turned him into a woman). Further, we should point out that Hellenistic culture also registers an 'absence of sight' apparently analogous to the one identified in the Jewish tradition: the 'absence of sight' of the nude goddess who does not immediately see the one who sees her is matched by the 'absence of sight' inflicted on Tiresias for seeing that which must not be seen. As for the mother's nudity in relation to the 'absence of sight', suffice it to note for now that Kerényi has connected Tiresias' blindness with Oedipus, the latter guilty of seeing his mother's nudity (and sexually joining with her). We stress these elements in order to clarify that a working hypothesis on the analysis of Daniel 13 as an epiphany of the third Rachel finds an opening in the comparison between Daniel 13 and extra-Jewish Hellenistic culture, provided this comparison takes into account the parallel occasions of mythological language documented in relation to the pre-Hellenistic religious phenomena forming the substratum both for the Elders in Daniel 13 and for Tiresias and Actaeon in the *Lauacrum Palladis*.

In this space that can comprise both the licit and the illicit as occasions of mythological language, the homology between the story of Susanna and that of Joseph and Potiphar's wife (and in particular its Hellenistic elaborations) presents itself as a tool for the analysis of Daniel 13 as a text geared to the juridical legitimization of mythological narrations that, from a juridical point of view, might have seemed elusive. In the same perspective, the elaborations undergone by the story of Joseph match juridical legitimization with a *per se* mythological correspondence through the refused union between Joseph and Potiphar's wife (*sui generis* 'mother' to Joseph) and the welcome union between Joseph and Aseneth (daughter to that 'mother'). Joseph's temptation (like Susanna's) corresponds to the forbidding / refusal of incest; but while in Joseph's story the union is finally achieved with a daughter (to that 'mother') who retains the extraneousness of the 'mother' to a legitimate sexual union with a Jew through the fact of being an idolatrous foreigner, in the story of Susanna the union *does not* take place. Aseneth's conversion to Judaism, legitimizing her union with Joseph, is homologous to the conversion of Joseph's temptation (on the part of Potiphar's wife, mother to Aseneth) into a legitimate relation with the mother. In Daniel 13, this transformation is not achieved—or rather, it is achieved only on a juridical level. The Elders are replaced, as judges to Susanna, by Daniel, as a true, legitimate judge to her. The entire mythological narration, its language being configured in juridical terms, translates the word 'judge' into the equivalent of 'sexual partner': illicit in the case of the Elders (who are 'judges' by definition and offer an illicit sexual union by mythological occasion), licit in the case of Daniel (who prophetically accedes to the function of 'judge' and, by mythological occasion, declares the mother juridically blameless, mythologically 'a virgin').

The wrong suffered by Bilhah thus appears as the space of mythological language protecting Rachel from all blame by opening her counterfigure to the risks, if not the guilt, of fornication. True, Bathsheba joins with David while awake, giving her consent to the illicit union, whereas Bilhah is caught asleep by Reuben ('and leaving her sleeping I departed'); but some connection with guilt seems to touch the figure of Bilhah, if only because she is found asleep and nude *through being drunk*: the stigma attached to drunkennes as a fault that can lead to more serious crimes is frequent in the Testaments of the Twelve Patriarchs, particularly in Judah, where it is directly connected to the latter's illicit unions with Bathshua and Tamar. Yet Bathsheba's sin is included in the category of crimes committed *bejad ramah* ('with raised hand', i.e. voluntarily), while the sin 'suffered' by Bilhah might be understood as one of those committed *bishegagah* ('unwittingly'), although case records of involuntary sins elaborated in the post-biblical era list as *bishegagah* exclusively those sins committed through ignorance or forgetfulness. There are no unilateral indications on sins committed while asleep, and in fact the relationship between the story of Susanna and the story of Joseph may be read as the relationship between two versions of incest with a mother who is *necessarily* innocent and *must refuse* or *be refused* according to whether the person tempted— Joseph or Susanna—will suffer the penal consequences of slander or not.

### 3. Questions of Onomastics

Daniel 13 opens with a topographical indication: 'There dwelt a Jew *in Babylon*, called Joakim'. This is the indication of a 'faraway', and if we wish to formulate some hypothesis on the use of non-Jewish cultural elements in the analysis of mythological language in Daniel 13 it will be useful to give preliminary consideration to how that text might present the relationship between 'near' and 'far', between 'familiar' (or possibly 'national') and 'foreign'.

Babylon, as such, is neither a Jewish nor a Greek space. From the point of view of the writing of Daniel 13, composed in Greek by a Jew, Babylon is, however, only a relatively foreign space.

It is a space in which the Jews lived, albeit in exile; and a space in which, during Hellenism, the language of the Greek *koiné* was doubtlessly circulating. The text of Daniel 13 is presumed to be the Greek version of a Hebrew or Aramaic original: since, however, this is only a hypothesis, and since not the least trace of the presumed non-Greek original remains, we can give but very little consideration to the fact that the story of Susanna might have been previously narrated in a language other than Greek. To limit ourselves to the Jews: those among them who engaged with Susanna's name, being bilingual in Hebrew and Greek, would have heard that name in exile and probably perceived it as a sound in which, in the land of exile, the Jewish and Greek cultural 'homelands' were joined.

Susanna's name (*Shoshanna*, 'lily') is a word in the Hebrew lexicon. Conradus Ikenius, in his brief essay *De lilio saronitico, emblematae sponsae* (Bremen 1728), had offered an early attempt to analyse the valency of this word, which denotes the lily in the Song of Songs (2:1–2) and in Hosea (14:6). As for post-biblical Jewish literature, in the Targum Sheni the groom's alter ego, Benaiah, sent by Solomon to welcome the Queen of Sheba, is the 'lily that grows by the water of the stream'; and *Shoshannat Yaakov* ('Lily of Jacob') is the title of the last section of the Piyyut of Asher Heni, recited morning and evening at Purim after the text of Esther's scroll.

With regard to the Greek cultural 'homeland' of the bilingual Jew who wrote Daniel 13 or read that text in the Hellenistic age, we should however bear in mind that the noun σοῦσον ('lily'), and the qualifier σούσινος ('of the lily'), both calques of the Hebrew (and generally West Semitic) form, had already become part of the Greek lexicon in the Hellenistic age. It is difficult to precisely determine in which epoch this noun and qualifier first appeared in Greek, and thus also to establish whether, for example, Aeschylus might already really have perceived the name of Susa (Σοῦσα in Greek) as 'City of the Lilies'. For an analysis of Daniel 13, it is first and foremost important to note that whoever might have written the story of Susanna in Greek separated the name of the lily from its earlier Greek form, λείριον, and at the same time positioned it as a noun that was by now Greek, *shoshanna*-σοῦσον, within the 'foreign' space of Babylon: it is beyond doubt that *Shoshanna* (whether written in Hebrew or Greek) would directly refer to *shoshanna* ('lily') not only for the author of the presumed Hebrew original but also for the author of Daniel 13. *Shoshanna* and σοῦσον thus ring out as 'lily', as both a Hebrew and a Greek sound, in the 'faraway' circumscribed by the words '[There dwelt a Jew] in Babylon'. However, in both its Hebrew and Greek sense, that sound, precisely because both Hebrew and Greek, was only relatively 'foreign' in Babylon, for the reasons mentioned—which should be considered in depth. (But before doing so, we should note that the joining of the Hebrew and Greek languages in the name of Susanna occurs, at least according to the documents available, in the Hellenistic era, and thus within a very diverse cultural environment, comprising, as well as the 'Babylon', 'Hebrew language' and 'Greek language' components, the 'Egyptian tradition' component, especially important to the specific area of Alexandrian Hellenism to which belong mythological materials such as those in the *Lauacrum Palladis*. In this respect, we should note that, thanks to the overriding of λείριον by σοῦσον, the sphere of *Shoshanna* also includes the essential oil of lily, the perfume we can see being manufactured in two Late Period Egyptian reliefs. Dioscorides [1:62–63] and Pliny [13.1] call it σοῦσινον and *susinum*, probably referring to its production in Semitic language countries; but this is the essential oil derived from the flower that has symbolized Upper Egypt since protohistory: in classical Egyptian, *swt > śwt* or *šm'w > šm'*; for this reason the oil was perhaps endowed with a particular sacred or magical value in the Egyptian tradition).

If we consider *Shoshanna*, in itself, as a Hebrew name-noun (with an autonomous Hebrew quality in a text like Daniel 13), the fact that it is heard 'in Babylon' as in a country that is only relatively foreign does not depend exclusively from Babylon being a place of residence for the Jews. As a land of exile, Babylon is a 'residence of exile', where the stress is on *exile* more than *residence*. Daniel 13, on the other hand, configures Babylon—as the stage set for the story of Susanna—as a not entirely foreign space of mythological language, if we accept 'Babylon' as homologous to the original space of mythological language in the Dan[i]el (*Dnil*) of the Ugaritic tradition, and the Daniel of the homonymous book in the Bible as directly connected with the Ugaritic Dan[i]el. This hypothetical homology opens the possibility of a connection between the Hellenistic *Shoshanna* and the Sumerian *ᵈShuẓianna*, 'the younger wife of Enlil, the wet nurse of Sin'. From a strictly philological point of view, the connection between *ᵈShuẓianna* and *Shoshanna* is far from obvious. And the connection between Susa as the 'city of lilies' and *Shoshanna* is as problematic, if not more. There is controversy even on the connection between the *shush* sound of the double ideogram used to write the name of the city and the two elements that compose it: Inanna (*nin*) and the 'cedar' (*erin*). There is no one answer, that is, on the attitude of Babylonian scribes relative to the connection between the *shush* sound and the breaking down of the corresponding ideogram into *nin* + *erin* (*ninni.erin* in Sumerian) = 'Inanna of the cedar': a singular toponym, to say the least, for a locality set in an area where—it seems—there have never been any cedars.

We are thus forced to proceed along an extremely tenuous track. We can presume—although no elements outside the text of Daniel 13 clearly prove it—that in the 'faraway' of Babylon, to a Hellenistic author and reader, the name of Susanna would be in a relationship of familiarity with Ugaritic and Elamite onomastics and mythological tradition; just like presumably (and this might be an even better founded assumption) the Daniel of the homonymous book was connected with the Ugaritic Dan[i]el. If we provisionally assume this twofold connection, Susanna and Daniel would constitute, from both the point of view of onomastics and that of more complex mythological contexts, two terms of coincidence between 'Babylon' (a *sui generis* Babylon including the memory of Ugaritic and Elamite cultural forms) and the Jews. It remains to be seen whether these hypotheses might possibly be confirmed—albeit partially and indirectly—within Daniel 13, or anyway within the scope of otherwise verified homologies between that 'within' and some other 'withins'.

The first point to be verified is the only partial foreignness of Susanna's name relative to 'Babylon' in the Greek outlook. As we have seen, the point that this was but a partial foreignness seems to be proved in the first place by the most elementary fact, i.e. by the circulation of the Greek language in 'Babylon' during Hellenism, and by the presence within *that* Greek language of the vocable 'σοῦσον'. If σοῦσον already was a point of coincidence between the Semitic 'faraway' and Greek culture, as the Greek calque of a Semitic form, the name 'Susanna' written in Greek in Daniel 13 created a further occasion of coincidence between Greekness and that 'faraway'. In order to delimit that coincidence, we can resort to analysing, on the one hand, the positioning of the σοῦσινον within Hellenistic Greek culture, and on the other hand the presumed homologies, at the level of mythological language, between Daniel 13 and the Hellenistic Greek texts connected to an older Greek tradition and showing the 'motif' of the spying of a bathing female figure and of the punishments suffered by those who spy.

As for the σοῦσινον, we do not have many elements available. Even the greatest specialist on ancient technology, R. J. Forbes, goes no further than listing 'lily oil' among the perfumes documented in the Near East and mentioning the sacred or magical value it presumably held in Egypt. When considering the possible connection between lily oil and the name of Susanna, we find instead elements for the reading of Daniel 13 specifically as a Hebrew text, albeit written in Greek. As can be observed, perfumed substances for uses other than the daily and the profane are connected to both Susanna's and Joseph's stories (although not directly to the part of Joseph's story—Joseph and Potiphar's wife—that we have connected to Susanna's). In Daniel 13, the name of Susanna is that of the flower from which an oil was distilled that presumably had a sacred or magical use in Egypt; also, the tree under which one of the two Elders declares he has seen Susanna fornicating with a young man is the mastic, *Pistacia lentiscus*, the source of the yellowish resin identified by some specialists with 'balm' (*ṣere* in Hebrew), and thus with a substance that was considered medicinal and endowed (for a Hellenistic Jew) with a sacred value, because used as a symbol of 'medicine' in sacred contexts (Jer 8:22; 46:11). In Genesis 37:25, the Ishmaelites to whom Joseph is sold by his brothers (according to this 'Elohist' portion of the text) bring into Egypt gum tragacanth (*neko't*), 'balm' (*ṣere*) and labdanum (*lot*). While gum tragacanth (assuming that is the correct translation of *neko't*) seems to have been used exclusively within the context of 'profane' medicine, 'balm' was, as we have seen, *also* sacred, and labdanum was burnt in the censers of Egyptian temples. The presence of aromatic substances endowed with sacred value in Daniel 13 and Genesis 37 might thus be connected to a sort of consecration of Susanna and of Joseph; however, firstly, the terms of this presumed consecration can at most be relatively direct only in the *Shoshanna*-σοῦσον-σοῦσινον connection; and, secondly, these would in any case be internal to a reading of Daniel 13 as a 'Jewish' text.

As for the homologies found—at the level of mythological language—between Daniel 13 and Hellenistic Greek texts like Callimachus' *Lauacrum Palladis*, it is possible to create a much more articulate hypothetical framework, mainly referred to pre-Hellenistic Greek traditions, to arrive at the interrelations between pre-Hellenistic

Greek mythological language and West Semitic mythological language. Assuming that the 'Babylon' of Daniel 13
is, as we have seen, a *sui generis* Babylon, including
within its 'faraway' (for the Hellenistic author and
reader) the memory of Ugaritic and Elamite cultural
forms, we cannot overlook the fact that a strand of
research culminating in Astour's *Hellenosemitica*[3] recognized as the origin of the figures of Tiresias and Actaeon
(thus precisely of the two mythological characters who,
in the *Lauacrum Palladis*, spy the epiphany of a nude
female figure at her bath) a cluster of West Semitic
mythological traditions. As regards Tiresias, the recognition of Semitic precedents or homologues is no longer
by now founded on onomastics (given the plausibility of
a Greek etymology of his name that rather weakens
Bérard's case for the Semitic *darash*, 'to consult an oracle'),
but derives from verification of other connections. In
the case of Actaeon, on the other hand, onomastics *also*
intervenes, given the plausibility of the hypothesis connecting the Greek name 'Ακταίων with *Aqht*, the name of
the main character in the Ugaritic poem in which Dan[i]el
also appears. 'Ακταίων supposedly is a derivation of one
of the more extended forms of *Aqht*, similar to Κάδμος
from the West Semitic *Qdm*, *Qdmn* and *\*Qdmyn*. Within
the scope of these hypotheses, it still remains to be seen
whether and how the actual text of Daniel 13, in the
'within' of its enclosed system, may give occasion to a
reading consistent with the reasons leading its Hellenistic
author and reader to find in it a connection between the
'faraway' of Babylon and their second, Greek, cultural
homeland.

---

3 Michael C. Astour, *Hellenosemitica* (Leiden: Brill, 1965) [Trans.]

## 4. Susanna 'at Her Bath': Oil on the Water

Daniel 13 says that Susanna went to bathe in the orchard 'for it was hot weather'. Susanna's bath is thus openly declared as profane, as well as quotidian ('[Susanna] went in on a time, as yesterday and the day before'—Dan 13:15). In sections 1 and 2 we proposed a hypothesis relative to the necessity, internal to the text, of this profane character of the bath. Such necessity can be further confirmed at the same time as we find confirmation of the connections between Susanna 'at her bath' and images from the non-Jewish mythological tradition: our entire hypothesis relative to that necessity, internal to the Hellenistic Jewish elaboration of Daniel 13, accordingly configures this necessity as the peculiarity of a *Jewish* generating of forms of mythological language (Susanna as the 'third Rachel'), and thus of a generating of forms that would find its limits—the modalities of its taking place—in differentiation from non-Jewish mythological languages in the 'faraway' of 'Babylon'—a space of indeterminacy relative to familiarity vs foreignness, just like the 'absence of sight' is a space of indeterminacy relative to licit vs illicit.

The connections between Susanna 'at her bath' and images from the non-Jewish mythological tradition are recognizable (with a remarkable margin of non-verifiable hypothesis) in the following nodes of mythological language:

(a) The Ugaritic context of the female deities connected with water in general, and in particular with springs, related to the presumed Semitic prototypes of the Greeks Tiresias and Actaeon.

(b) The 'healing' quality that often seems typical of these female deities and is associated with their frequently maternal character. Hence a widening of the presumed maternal character of Susanna as a 'third Rachel'—not because Susanna becomes a 'healer', but because the differentiation of Susanna from Ugaritic figures may be configured as a reversion of the 'healing' into juridically prosecuted guilt.

(c) As a corollary to the above: the possibility that a connection between *Shoshanna* and $^{d}Shuzianna$ might be operating for the Jewish Hellenistic author and reader of Daniel 13, given the fact that $^{d}Shuzianna$ was 'nurse' to Sin as Bilhah was to Joseph. Hence Susanna's responsibility to be mother to those (the Elders) who, being her sons but also unable to be her sons (*Elders* because 'old'), must not sexually join with her: Reuben joins with Bilhah, but Joseph does not join with Potiphar's wife.

(d) The presence within pre-Hellenistic Greek mythological tradition of figures such as Tiresias and Actaeon, which a Hellenistic text (the *Lauacrum Palladis*) connects with the spied bath of a female figure. The presumed connection of these figures to non-Greek (West Semitic) forms of mythological language.

(e) The presence of a figure, Dan[i]el, possibly correlated with the Daniel of the homonymous book, and which, in its first identity, appears in the 'Poem of Aqth' susceptible to generative steps possibly giving rise to Actaeon.

(f) The presence of the bath as a ritual act in the environment of pre-Hellenistic Greek cults or Hellenistic initiation and mysteric rites that are in fact documented in the Hellenistic Romances; the function of such baths *also* in view of a regeneration of the virginity of a mother figure.

(g) The analogy between Genesis 35:22 (Reuben and Bilhah) and *Iliad* 9:445–56 (the story of Phoenix), suggesting the hypothesis of a West Semitic background for a 'Greek' character whose name recalls 'Phoenicia'.

(h) The presence in Canaanite mythology (or rather, in what presumably is the Hittite version of a Canaanite mythological narration) of a stepmother, Ashertu, who attempts to seduce her stepson, the 'Storm God' (Baal), and, offended by his refusal, weeps for seven years, during which the gods (and perhaps men as well) are afflicted by a singular scourge: they drink hugely, but are always thirsty—it is as if they had been left without water.

A hypothesis taking into account the possible presence of traces of these elements in the 'Babylon' of Daniel 13 can lead us to recognize in Susanna 'at her bath', seen as the 'third Rachel', the faraway place where, for the bilingual Jew of Hellenism, the lily *Shoshanna*, oil of lily, floats on water, not for ritual reasons, but because oil always, ordinarily, floats on water (*Shoshanna* stepped into the water 'for it was hot weather'); and, also, the faraway place where the *Shoshanna* is 'oil of lily' endowed with special ritual prerogatives, and in her floating on water gives rise to forms within a space and a 'matter' (the 'layer' of mythological language) susceptible to taking on any form, since 'Babylon' is the space of indeterminacy relative to familiarity vs foreignness, to (familiar) 'forms' vs (non-familiar, foreign) 'non-forms'. The forms determined by that floating on water are *naked* forms, devoid of any clothing or ornaments other than their pure limits with respect to water, and this nakedness accomplishes its epiphany in the 'faraway' that is 'absence of sight', a space of indeterminacy relative to licit vs illicit, in which the naming of naked forms as a whole is posited as a naming of what can but must not be seen. Susanna's nudity can but must not be seen. The nakedness of forms created by oil poured into a cup of water is what can be seen, what the diviner *must* see in order to know the future, according to the lecanomanctic practices of Mesopotamia, and perhaps of Egypt, Greece. But the outsider *must* not see them, for he does not *know how* to see them. The homology between Daniel (Dan 13) and Joseph (Gen 44) can thus be configured as a homology between the fact that Daniel, unlike the Elders, has both the power and the knowledge to see the nudity of Susanna, innocent in the water into which she has stepped, just like Joseph has both the power and the knowledge to see and to divine through the naked forms taken by oil on the water in the cup he pretends his brothers stole from him—the brothers who once sold him into slavery to the Ishmaelites, merchants of aromatic oils and resins.

# When Kerényi Diverted Me from Jung

EDITOR'S NOTE

Relatively undisguised in the folds of the interview format, 'self-portrait' finally makes its decisive appearance in the following text, one of the last left by Jesi. We do not know who the author of the questions might have been, but we can be certain that Jesi did, if not rewrite them, at least rework them. In words that closely recall the beginning of his essay on the Story of Susanna, he returns to mythology as a language and positions the 'mythological machine model' at the centre of his practice. Retracing his beginnings, when, aged fifteen, he published his first essay in the prestigious review of the Oriental Institute of the University of Chicago, he recalls encountering Kerényi and distancing himself from Jung's influence, dwelling especially on his own method of knowledge by composition. The tutelary deities of his late research, always poised between knowledge and narration, were Benjamin and Bachofen. Owing to Jesi's untimely death on 17 June 1980, his 'Benjaminian' study *Traduzione e duplicità dei linguaggi*,[1] and his 'Salgari',[2] i.e. the annotated translation of Bachofen's *Mutterrecht*, were both left unfinished. A few chapters of the latter have remained in the Einaudi translation;[3]

---

1 The unfinished text was kept among Jesi's letters in a small folder with 9 typed and numbered pages. It was posthumously published in *Cultura Tedesca* 12 (December 1999).

2 The reference is to Emilio Salgari (1862–1911), a hugely prolific Italian writer of popular travel adventure novels and science fiction. [Trans.]

3 Johann Jakob Bachofen, *Il matriarcato. Ricerca sulla ginecocrazia del mondo antico nei suoi aspetti religiosi e giuridici* (Giulio Schiavoni ed., Furio Jesi partial trans. and introd.) (Turin: Einaudi, 1988) / *Myth, Religion and Mother Right*: *Selected Writings of J. Bachofen* (Ralph

and much of it is referenced in the work of genius we know as his *Bachofen*, published posthumously in 2005.[4]

The interview was first published, edited by this writer, in *Alias* 30 (28 July 2007): 21.

---

Manheim trans., Joseph Campbell introd.) (Princeton, NJ: Princeton University Press, 1973).

4 Furio Jesi, *Bachofen* (Andrea Cavalletti ed.) (Turin: Bollati Boringhieri, 2005).

# When Kerényi Diverted Me from Jung

QUESTION. Your first essay, published more than twenty years ago, was about a Hellenistic scroll,[1] and the subject of your first book was Ancient Egyptian pottery.[2] The study of archaeology and ancient civilizations thus marked the beginning of your journey as a theorist. How does one arrive at the science of myth through study of the ancient world?

ANSWER. Back then, I certainly had not set out for myself a calculated plan that would take me from papyrology and archaeology to the science of myth. That's just what happened, and I can only speak with hindsight, through which I note that many of those early studies helped put before my eyes or in my hands, helped me read, touch and measure, materials that today we wish could enable us to think our way back to the people and cultures that produced them.

The science of myth, as I understand it, finds itself in an analogous situation: we have at our disposal 'mythological materials' that can be weighed, photographed, philologically analysed; regarding myth, not

---

1 Furio Jesi, 'Notes sur l'édit dionysiaque de Ptolémée IV Philopator', *Journal of Near Eastern Studies* 15(4) (October 1956): 236–40. [Trans.]
2 Furio Jesi, *La ceramica egizia* (Turin: Saie, 1958). [Trans.]

only do we know nothing at all, but out of logical consistency declare we cannot know anything. The archaeologist circumscribes a space in which a certain culture may well have existed, but is unable to set foot in that space; the mythologist circumscribes a mechanism that may well be moved by myth, but is not in a position to state that myth exists.

For me, working with archaeology has also meant travelling—through Greece, Turkey, Egypt, or through the findings of museums. These travels, and at times long stays, in 'ancient lands' have meant repeating—but turning it into its exact opposite—the experience of eighteenth-century travellers: travelling, that is, in order to learn to *not* know the world and to collect fragments of it that hark back to nothing but themselves, 'mythological materials'—or as Bachofen would have said, 'symbols resting upon themselves'.

QUESTION. In your view, what is the difference between *science of myth* and *science of mythology*? And in particular, what is your concept of the *science of myth*?

ANSWER. If by *myth* we mean that 'something' alluded to by the mythological machine as to the existence of its presumed immoveable mover; and if by *mythological materials* we mean the machine's historically verifiable products, then the science of myth is a typical science of what is historically not there, whereas the science of mythology is the study of mythological materials as such. The science of myth, in my view, tends to be actualized as a science of reflections about myth, and thus as an analysis of the various modalities of non-knowledge of myth. The science of mythology, consisting as it does of the study of mythological materials 'as such', tends to be actualized first and foremost as a science of the workings of the mythological machine, and thus as an analysis of the internal, autonomous linguistic circulation that makes those materials mythological. I use the word *mythology* precisely to indicate that linguistic circulation and the materials that document it.

QUESTION. From *Letteratura e mito* (1968) to *Materiali mitologici* (1979), you have acknowledged the direct influence of Károly Kerényi on your formation as a scholar of mythology. What do you think is the most vibrant part of Kerényi's output, and which aspect of it remains most relevant to the theoretical activity you are currently engaged in?

ANSWER. Kerényi's work has its own basic compactness of contradictions warranting its vitality. In outlining what I think I learnt mainly from him, I should go back to the previous question. For me, considering mythology as an internal, autonomous linguistic circulation peculiar to certain materials means positioning myself outside important and perhaps prevalent currents in contemporary linguistics, that view so-called mythological materials solely as *texts* which are qualified as 'mythological' simply because, through an error of method, the observer remains hypnotized by one of their numberless possible senses, giving it preference as if it were endowed with intrinsic objectivity. I derive the notion of such 'error of method' from Kerényi and from his anthropology, with which I am in agreement, at least from this point of view.

I do not believe in the existence of myth (I use the word 'believe' in its strongest sense, because this would properly be an act of faith); but I am convinced that for me, today, the best way of positioning myself in front of any mechanisms and productions (both my own and others', whether ancient or contemporary) is to recognize in some of those productions a language not reducible to any other, absolutely autonomous, 'resting upon itself' (Bachofen), endowed with other features definable through extremely vague approximations if—as is inevitable when *defining* them—one resorts to another language.

It follows that I continue to see the Kerényian analogy between mythology and music as appropriate, and that I have stressed (or at least made more explicit than Kerényi deemed opportune) the Kerényian criterion by which each production in this field is truly scientific if the critique—in the Kantian sense of the word—enacted within its scope is first and foremost a self-critique. From Kerényi I have learnt the possibility of perceiving the weight of mythology, the necessity internal to mythological materials, without for this having to believe in myth as in a 'something' that 'is dynamic, has a power, takes hold of life and shapes it' (Walter F. Otto); also, the sense of distance from the mythology or mythologies of the ancients ('There's many a slip between the cup and the lip . . . ')[3], which does not however reduce awareness of that faraway object as concerning us intimately and

---

3 See Kerényi's 'Prolegomena' to Carl Gustav Jung and Károly Kerényi, *Science of Mythology*: *Essays on the Myth of the Divine Child and the Mysteries of Eleusis* (R. F. C. Hull trans.) (London: Routledge and Kegan Paul, 1951). [Trans.]

personally. I do not think I *know the mythology* of the ancients or the moderns; I think the scientific character of my approach to mythological materials and reflections on myth consists, first and foremost, of the existential free choice subtending the words 'for me, today, the best way of positioning myself in front of . . . '.

QUESTION. A quick-fire question: What influence did Jung's work have on you? And also: Are there any parts of Jung's work from which you feel you might be able to draw any methodological teachings—or perhaps something more?

ANSWER. In the late Fifties, when I began to study mythological materials, symbols and methodological proofs of the science of myth, Jung's texts excited me very much, more so than Kerényi's. 'Collective unconscious', 'archetype', 'mandala', sounded like words of wisdom to me. In 1957, while staying at the Monastery of the Transfiguration, in the Meteora region of Thessaly, to attempt a study of Neoplatonism in relation with Graeco-orthodox religiosity, I had with me books by Leo Frobenius and Vladimir Propp, and was trying to resolve the contradictions between them through Jung. My early writings in this field—'Le connessioni archetipiche' and 'Sul fatto miracoloso'[4]—are in many respects Jungian, although even then I felt a certain unease towards the 'archetype' as the mould to a fully rounded figure, and was trying to remedy that through the 'archetypal connections' model: linguistic constants, as I would say

---

4 Jesi, 'Le connessioni archetipiche' (1958); and 'Sul fatto miracoloso', *Archivio internazionale di etnografia e preistoria* 2 (1959): 21–9. [Trans.]

today—rigid compositional norms rather than organic figures in a gallery of portraits.

Later, little by little, Kerényi became the *magister*, and since the time when I began to know him personally and to become more deeply involved in studying him, he has taken me further and further away from Jung. Precisely those 'archetypal connections' that, with the moralistic 'calling' of my 16–17 years, I had judged as gnoseological 'values', have now become a sort of emotional indecency, like walking naked down the street— something that is not done or said, even if it must be taken into account when writing one's self-portrait.

Later still, things became even more complicated: I like it, don't like it—I can't say I like it or don't like it . Today, right now, I can say that in Jung I don't much like anything implying an 'I know . . . '—not because one cannot say so without being a perfectly proper person, but because it's a bit of a mess.

QUESTION. You have been working since 1969 on a near 'mythological' first Italian edition of Bachofen's *Mutterrecht*, forthcoming from Einaudi. Can you tell us what Bachofen represented, and represents, for you?

ANSWER. To get away with a *bon mot*, I could answer that Bachofen has for many years been my Salgari. Certainly, most of Bachofen's work constitutes a splendid mythological novel. There's some *writing* in there—the taste for knowledge by composition that Walter Benjamin celebrated with the words 'a scientific prophecy'. In Bachofen there is none of the awareness of clairvoyance attributed to him in the early decades of the twentieth century by the right wing of the Bachofen Renaissance, but rather a patrician assuredness (and a grim mood besides) in composing to one's own engaged and solitary taste the numberless materials of one's collection. In *Essay on the Tomb Symbolism of the Ancient* (1859), those materials are, first and foremost, appraised as 'symbols resting upon themselves'. In the *Mutterrecht*, with a process peculiar to the historical novel (which is by its nature mythological novel), the compositional praxis determines two processes: the world as a collection of symbols resting upon themselves is summoned thanks to the presence of witnesses that are the logical categories of the law, identified with the structures of knowability of history; whereas the knowability (through juridical structures) of history is summoned by the weight of a collection of symbols—a specific weight acquired by that collection through being arbitrarily ordered in a certain way by the judge.